WORDPRESS FOUNDATIONS

BY JASON ANNAS

EnlightenedWebMastery.com

Proudly Present

WORDPRESS FOUNDATIONS

BY JASON ANNAS

A comprehensive up to date workbook on

getting started with WordPress.

WordPress Foundations

Presented by:

EnlightenedWebMastery.com

For general information on our other products, please visit our website at **www.EnlightenedWebMastery.com.**

Last edited on February 19th, 2009

Table of Contents

Chapter 1

Introduction to the book

First I would like to thank you for taking a chance, and purchasing this book. I hope this book provides you with the answers that you seek, and get you online as quickly as possible.

Let me tell you about the book first so you know how to use it best to reach your goals.

This book is structured as a workbook / reference book. My first goal is to get you online right away, the right way. So when you first go through the book, if you do not have a blog yet, I want you to follow along with the book in real time.

As you read a chapter, I want you to take notes on a piece of paper, or write in the margins of this book. I recommend having a highlighter, a pen, and some post-it flags handy while going through the book.

At the beginning of each chapter I will tell you about the chapter, what it's about, and what I want you to pay attention to. At the end of each chapter you will see a summary of the topics covered, as well as the action steps that I want you to follow.

If you currently have a blog, and it's not at the level you would like, I want you to go through the book, and take note of what is discussed. Pay careful attention to the workflows presented, as well as the various tips and tricks scattered throughout the chapter.

Think to yourself, how can I apply this information?

After you've read the book, and your site is up, you need to approach the book with a different mindset.

WordPress Foundations as a Reference

After you've read the book you may wish to revisit the book to find an answer to your current dilemma.

The best way to do this is read the table of contents; skip to that part of the book (if you tagged the book as I suggested in the previous section, finding the content will be that much easier) and search for the solution. You do not need to re-read the entire chapter, instead, check the parts that you highlighted and tagged, and follow those steps.

WordPress.com or WordPress.org

I'm presenting this book as if you're new to WordPress. I recommend setting up a WordPress.com account first (because it is free, you can toy around and not mess anything up, and it provides the perfect learning environment).

Once you're comfortable with the WordPress platform, I highly recommend signing up for a domain name (GoDaddy.com is great) then get a hosting account to host your website (imountain.com, hostgator.com, dreamhost.com, mediatemple.com are all great places) and then start using WordPress.org to power your website.

The reason for this is WordPress.org offers much more than the free version at WordPress.com. With .org you can design your own theme or install one of the many freely distributed ones.

You have full control over the look and functionality, and you also own the domain name. When someone visits your site, they will see yourname.com not yourname.wordpress.com.

If you know you will be hosting your blog at your website (yourname.com or yourcompany.com) then I recommend reading chapter 22 first, to learn how to setup and install WordPress.org with your hosting account.

I should note, when you are looking for a hosting provider, many of them offer "1-click Installs" for WordPress. If your hosting provider offers this, then leave chapter 22 alone and use that option. All you have to do is push a button, and WordPress is installed and configured for you. If that is not an option for you, then Chapter 22 will show you how to install WordPress in under 5 minutes.

Topics Covered in WordPress Foundations

In this book I will take you by the hand, assuming very little, and get you started blogging in the shortest amount of time possible.

Chapter 1 - Introduction to the book

You will learn how to setup a freely hosted account at wordpress.com, and use this for your main platform (I will focus mainly on this throughout the book, and have a separate section devoted to self hosting, I highly recommend using the self-hosted option for your site, and to think of wordpress.com as your "training wheels").

What's In The Book

Chapter 1 introduces you to the book, and shows you how we will be proceeding.

Chapter 2 covers blogging basics, you will learn what a blog is, the different "types" of blogs that you can create, and learn some "Blogging Terminology".

Chapter 3 we cover which version of WordPress is right for you, discussing the options, and how they differ.

Chapter 4 is where we get started using WordPress. You learn about how to setup your account, how to login, and other tasks you will be required to perform.

Chapter 5 introduces you to the dashboard, which is how you manage your entire blog. I will be teaching you the interface, how to navigate around it, and how to view your stats.

Chapter 6 we move into setting up your blog, you will learn how to edit your profile, setup your personal options, how to update your name, configure various settings for your blog. You will also learn how to enable comment moderation to stop spam in its tracks, as well as how to adjust the privacy settings of your blog.

Chapter 7 delves into writing posts. You will learn and master the writing panel. We will go through and write our "First Post" and then we will learn some advanced concepts to apply when using tags or categories. I will share with you some very valuable shortcuts that can save you some time. We will also cover how to use the HTML editor, and how to publish your posts.

Chapter 8 covers creating Pages. These are different than posts, this chapter discusses those differences, and teaches you when and how to use each.

Chapter 9 covers how to apply a theme. I will also personally go over and critique 5 themes that I think are really strong to use for your blog. This is a very valuable chapter, and will have your website looking better almost instantly.

Chapter 10 goes into Widgets, you will learn what they are, how to add them to your site and more.

Chapter 11 goes into the extras and upgrades you can get by using wordpress.com

Chapter 12 covers the process of adding a logo to your site using the Custom Image Header function, things to look out for, and how best to proceed

Chapter 13 continues from chapter 12 and we cover how to put your new logo on your site.

Chapter 14 teaches you all you need to know about comments. You will learn why you should enable comments, how to view your comments, how to go about moderating those comments and much more.

Chapter 15 is where the real fun begins. This chapter is all about adding multimedia to your website. We will be covering how to embed video, including youtube, how to add mp3's, adding photos and other graphics, as well as how to embed PDF's. I will also go over some techniques you should keep in mind with how to manage your Media Library.

Chapter 16 covers some more advanced topics. You're going to learn how to manage your posts and pages. You will learn about the more tag, how to use it, strategies to keep in mind. You will also learn some tips and tricks on how to edit and delete your content.

Chapter 17 delves much deeper into categories and tags. You will learn the difference between them, how to create categories and tags. You will learn how to delete them, how to manage them, and how to convert tags to categories, and categories to tags.

Chapter 18 teaches you how to add users to your site, so you can split the work up between multiple people.

Chapter 19 covers password protection. Learn how it works, why you might want to use it, and why you might not.

Chapter 20 goes over your blogroll, you will learn what a blogroll is, and how to manage it.

Chapter 21 covers some of the most important material in the book, and that is Maintenance. Once you have your site up and online, there are certain things you really need to do to ensure your blog is up to date, that search engines can find you, and to make sure your not getting spammed. This is a chapter you will be referencing for years to come.

Chapter 22 covers tips and techniques for bloggers who are going to be self-hosting. You will learn where to get the program, and learn how to install it in under 5 minutes! We will cover what is required, how to create the mysql databases and users, how to get thousands of free themes, and how to install them.

Chapter 23 covers where you need to go after reading this book. How best to proceed.

What you need to follow along with this book

To follow along with this book, all you need is a valid email address and this book. I show you how to do everything using WordPress.com. As the platforms are very similar, the concepts and techniques taught do apply to WordPress.org as well.

If you will be using the WordPress.org solution, you will need a hosting account, a domain name, and a FTP client (to upload files from your computer to your server).

I recommend using Filezilla as a FTP program, as it is fully featured, free, and available on all platforms.

If you would like some more free software that you can use to power your blog or website, I recommend checking out "A Webmasters Essential Tools Part 1" which is an article I wrote (which you can find by typing in the URL below) that shows several valuable yet free tools that can help you when creating your website.

enlightenedwebmastery.com/webmasters-essential-tools-part-1

As far as technical skills are required, all you need to know is how to check your email, read this book, follow along, be dedicated, and most of all, have fun!

Feedback

Please feel free to send me feedback. I want to know what you think about the book, the parts you liked, or disliked, how much it helped you, and what you would like to learn in the future. Help me help you. You can do so by visiting my website and clicking the "Contact Me" link.

If there is anything you would like to learn more about, do not hesitate to ask, if you have a question, chances are others do too. I will do my best to help you, and possibly post a tutorial on my website to help you and others right away.

Your Secret Weapon

When I wrote this book and designed the course, I had a very specific goal in mind. Other books that cover WordPress throw a lot of stuff at you, and it can be hard to understand what's important, and what you should pay attention to.

That's why throughout this book I try to cover "exactly" what you need to know, and I don't spend a lot of time covering certain features and topics.

I think this is very beneficial, as you're not reading stuff you do not need to know right away. However, there is more information about WordPress and blogging that you indeed do need to know.

Introducing EnlightenedWebMastery.com

Enlightened WebMastery is your secret weapon.

When you visit my website, you will find countless free tutorials covering more advanced parts of WordPress. Things you need to know, but are not essential to getting started with using WordPress.

I implore you to visit the website and start taking advantage of this valuable information. My goal is to provide short and quick tutorials (with video training) that teach you how to do something that can seem pretty difficult at first, and break it down into something that you can do yourself right away.

To get the full effect of the website, and get access to the special reports, bonus videos, and more, you need to sign up for my free newsletter at enlightenedwebmastery.com/newsletter

Once you're on the newsletter, you get lots of free stuff. I'm providing valuable reports that are too big to put on my website, exclusive videos, as well as advanced peaks at what's going on and what's happening (along with the monthly newsletter that you do NOT want to miss).

Some of the articles and videos currently located on the website are:

How To Install WordPress Plugins (This article shows you how to install a plugin right from WordPress's dashboard, so you no longer need to unzip a file and upload, this is a very powerful new feature, and I show you how to do it step by step with a video.)

Advanced YouTube Embedding Techniques (In this article I show you how to embed High Quality and High Definition Videos into your blog from YouTube, as well as how to turn off "related videos" how to "autoplay" your videos, and how to adjust the size of the videos.)

How To Make Your WordPress Site iPhone Friendly (In this article I show how to make sure your WordPress site looks "right" on an iPhone or iPod in less than 2 minutes.)

I also cover other topics such has how to fix common WordPress errors like the Redirection Loop, How To Stop Self Pingbacks, and more.

I have a video that shows you how to backup your blog, as well as how to update your blog to the latest version of WordPress.

I teach Search Engine Optimization training. With this material you will learn how to get listed in the search engines quickly, you will learn how to setup your WordPress Permalinks the right way (with video), and so much more.

You really owe it to yourself to checkout the site. I also recommend subscribing to the RSS feed while you're so you know the instant new content is available.

If you are new to RSS then I encourage you to checkout my article called **"What is RSS and How Do I Use It?"** and "**Google Reader Introduction With Tips**".

enlightenedwebmastery.com/what-is-rss-and-how-do-i-use-it

enlightenedwebmastery.com/google-reader-introduction-with-tips

Chapter 1 Summary

In this chapter we went over a brief tour of the book and the topics covered. I introduced you to Enlightened WebMastery, and explained how to get the most out of this book.

In the next chapter you will learn more about blogging in general, as well as hone in on what type of blog you wish to create.

Chapter 1 Action Steps

- Get out a pen a highlighter and some post it notes before you read the next chapter.
- Make sure you have something to write on (paper notebook, or the book).
- Visit EnlightenedWebMastery.com, signup for the free newsletter and subscribe to the RSS feed.
- Turn off any possible distractions (web browser, TV, phone, etc, so you can focus on the book and designing your blog).

Chapter 2

Blogging Basics

Introduction to chapter 2

In this chapter you're going to learn about the different types of blogs that are out there, and the differences between them.

There is another style of blog that I do not cover in this chapter that is called "Magazine" the way it works (check CNN, New York Times) is the website is static, meaning the look and feel stays the same, but the content is always changing. To learn more about magazine styles you should checkout my website for more information.

I should warn you, as of this writing, you cannot choose a magazine style theme when using wordpress.com (so if you're interested in this type of platform and layout, I highly recommend choosing WordPress.org as your blogging platform.)

As you are reading this chapter, I want you to think about what kind of blog you want to create. Do you want to create a photoblog? A news blog? A personal or professional blog?

Keep this thought in the back of your mind while you read this chapter, when you reach the end of the chapter, I want you to have a firm grasp on what kind of blog you wish to create.

So what exactly is a "blog" anyway?

A "Blog" is a shortening of the words web and log. For you and me, it's a website for personal or professional use, maintained by one person, that is updated frequently, and is set up in such a way that other people on the internet can read it, and comment on the material.

A blog can contain not only text, but also audio, video, and photos. Blogs started out being used as journals, and they still are, a place where you can share your thoughts and what you're doing with the world at large.

Please be aware, that blogging is a public medium, and as such, you do not necessarily want to publish your most private thoughts.

It's a good idea to not post things that might come back around and bite you in the future.

These can lead to a series of problems. Many people have gotten fired, divorced, or worse, due to what they wrote on their blogs.

What are the different types of blogs out there?

There are many different types of blogs out there. Most of them fall under a few categories. The main ones being as followed:

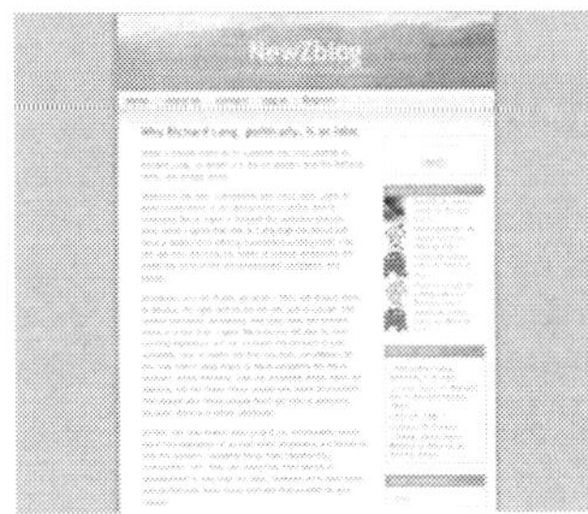

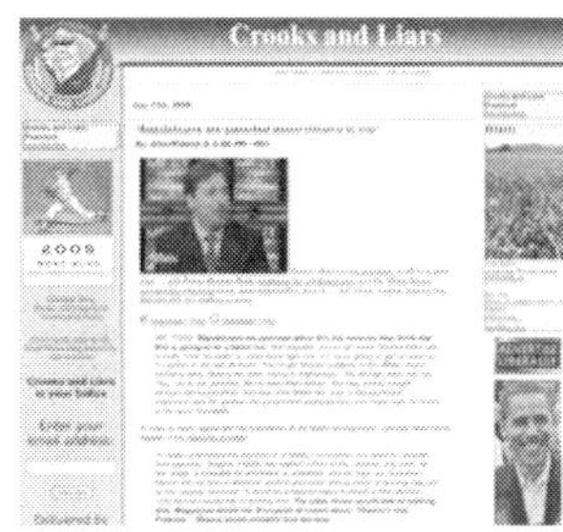

(1) Normal (2) Photo (3) Video

The Typical Blog

This is what you normally find on the Internet. The design is nice and clean, it's easy to find what you're looking for and (for the blogger) it's very easy to setup and maintain.

The major benefits of creating this type of blog are:

- It's easy to maintain
- Readers are used to it
- It's easy for them to find what they're looking for

The Photo Blog

Another popular type of blog that is very common on the Internet is what's known as a "Photo Blog".

The benefit of having a photo blog is you can share your latest images with the world. These can be paintings, 3D renders, photography, 2D renders, images of sculpture, logo designs, or anything. The point is showcasing your work in a very visual way.

If you're wanting to show other people's images, you need to be aware of the copyrights for that particular image, and contact the owner prior to posting if you are unclear.

One thing to consider when creating a Photo Blog is, photos are large. The file sizes can be quite big, and the more people that view your site, the more bandwidth they consume.

This is a problem because, if you're paying for a hosting service (especially a shared hosting service) or using a free hosting account, you have bandwidth limitations (going over that limit can lead to you getting suspended from that host, or you having to pay additional money). A smart alternative is to host your images with another service and then embed those images into your blog.

Some services for storing your images online include: Zoomr, Flickr, Google's Picasa Web, imageshack.us or SmugMug.

If your site is a business site, I recommend either using Flickr, hosting the images yourself (chances are you have a high end hosting package) or my personal favorite, using Amazon's S3 service (this costs pennies a month to host massive amounts of data, it is literally the deal of a lifetime.)

If you want to learn more about Amazon S3 you should checkout their website and checkout my website for an in-depth article on Amazon S3 and how to use it.

The Video Blog

Last on the list is a video blog. People use video blogs in many different ways to serve a variety of purposes.

If you're an actor you can post readings and clips of you acting and use that for your promotion.

If you teach people how to cook, you can make quick videos and show them on your blog.

You can checkout Hulu.com as an example of showing TV shows on for free (you can also embed those videos onto your blog if you want), the dailyshow has a blog that shows the latest episodes of the daily show, and you can view those for free.

Other people post their favorite videos from youtube on their blog (like music videos, how-to's, funny clips) and that is their entire blog.

If you want to post your own videos to your website, you need to use WordPress.org, and I recommend using Amazon s3 to store your videos (they need to be compressed into .flv format) all of this I cover on my website as it is outside the scope of this book.

However, if you want to share your videos with the world, you can upload your videos to YouTube (for free) and then you can embed them on both your WordPress.org site and on WordPress.com (I cover this in a later chapter as well as on my site).

The Combination Blog

What I mean by combination is, the site has text posts, posts that are images, and posts that have video. The site does what it thinks is necessary.

This is what most blogs end up doing. Not every blog is focused on one aspect, some focus on multiple aspects.

If you checkout the example blog I setup for this book (TheTVReview.com) you will see that it is a combination of each.

When you click the picture banner, you will see a video, when you read the article you will see a lot of text, along with images.

If you visit enlightenedwebmastery.com, I have posts that have just text, posts that have text and pictures, and posts that have text, pictures, and video.

I mention this only to say, it's ok to incorporate these pieces together. Most people will be using "The Combination Blog" and the "Normal Blog" for their sites.

Blogging Terminology

If you are going to be a blogger, you must know a few common terms, else you'll be pulling your hair out with frustration.

At the heart of any blog are its posts. When you write something on your blog, that is a post. When you post something on your blog, WordPress creates something called a **permalink**, which is a fancy term for a permanent link to your post. You can give this URL how to anyone to they can then view that specific post.

When you write a post, (provided you have **comments** enabled), someone can **comment** on your blog. What this means is underneath your post, you will see a comments section. Anyone on the Internet will be able to post a comment about your post. It's up to you if you want this functionality on your blog or not. Some do, some don't. Most successful blogs have comments enabled. This is a great way to form a community, and encourages people to return to your site. With WordPress, you can disable the ability to comment on a post-by-post basis.

Another term you may not be familiar with is **Trackbacks**.

The way trackbacks works are, you write a post on your blog, then another blogger reads that post and decides to comment on it on their blog so their readers can benefit. So they post a "trackback" (which WordPress does automatically by linking to a blog) to your post.

Under that post you will notice a new comment that looks like:

[...] various text here [...]

The "..." mean there is something before or after this comment. You should be aware that spammers abuse this system to advertise on your blog. So you may want to keep checking on your comments so you can stop this if you are getting spammed.

Another recent term is **RSS**. What RSS does is allow someone to subscribe to your site, and read your material from their RSS reader, opposed to visiting your website. You can learn more about RSS by checking out my article called "**What Is RSS And How Do I Use It?**" which is located on my blog at:

enlightenedwebmastery.com/what-is-rss-and-how-do-i-use-it

Chapter 2 Summary

In this chapter we went over a brief tour of the different types of blogs, and a few blogging terms you should be familiar with.

Chapter 2 Action Steps

Now that you have read this chapter, I want you to do the following

- Choose which type of blog you wish to create
- Which will best suit your goals?
- What is the purpose of your blog going to be? To showcase your images? Writing talent? Promote a product, brand, or service?
- Take 5 minutes, write out your goals and figure out what you want to achieve. Think hard about which format will best help you reach your outcome, so you get a better idea as to what kind of blog to create.

Chapter 3

Choosing which version of WordPress to use

Introduction to chapter 3

The goal of this chapter is to determine which version of WordPress is right for you. I will mainly be focusing on WordPress.org VS WordPress.com.

While reading this chapter, think which version is right for you. WordPress.com is free and you can use right now (which can be great to start learning WordPress, but if you ever want to go to your own domain name, you will loose readers and content by switching to your own custom hosting solution.)

So while you're reading this, think hard about which way you want to go. I encourage you to checkout WordPress.com first, and get used to it, but I recommend hosting your final site using WordPress.org.

The Different WordPress Services

WordPress offers four different "classes" of service. The first three are free; the fourth is for large companies who need support. That version will not be covered in this book.

WordPress.com - This is the version we will be covering in exhaustive detail. This version is hosted at wordpress.com, as such; you don't need to pay anything. It's a free turnkey solution.

You go to *wordpress.com*, create an account and your running (I will show you how to do this soon).

Wordpress.org - This version will be covered here as well, but not extensively, as the individual parts that make this so different could cover multiple books. With this version you need 2 things: A host (one that supports WordPress, PHP and MySQL) this usually costs money, and a domain name. An example name is *you.com.*

WordPress MU - You get this at *http://mu.wordpress.org.* The benefit of using this is it allows you to create a network of blogs all housed under a single domain name. This is not meant for individual users; rather, it's intended for large corporations, which have multiple blogs (thousands even) on the same domain, using the same server. We will not be covering this version of WordPress, as it's not something most people will use.

WordPress KWEE - This is the Enterprise edition, known as the "KnowNow WordPress Enterprise Edition." It's only available for Fortune 500 companies. It competes with other enterprise class platforms, and thus not for you or me. We will also not be covering this version.

What are the major differences?

In this book, we are focusing mainly on wordpress.com. Wordpress.com is a self-hosted service. It's like your email account. You do not pay for the name (Gmail, Yahoo, Hotmail, etc), you don't pay for the hosting (unless your using a premium account, and even then your not administering the host), you just get to use the service, and enjoy all that it entails.

For self-hosting (WordPress.org) you need a domain which costs about 10$, and hosting which costs a similar amount or more. Hosting usually incurs a monthly fee, so you'll need to pay for this each month.

To start using the self-hosted version, you need to upload WordPress to your server, create a database, a username, and install WordPress and set it up.

If you're going to use WordPress.org you need a hosting account.

I recommend HostGator, Dreamhost, iMountain, and MediaTemple for hosting. These are places I have used in the past and can recommend.

Benefits of WordPress.org vs WordPress.com

WordPress.com

Pros:

No Cost, No Experience, Can be online in less than 30 seconds.

Cons:

Limited amount of themes, no plugins, your site is "you.wordpress.com" opposed to "you.com", you cannot customize the look (other than the provided themes, unless you pay to edit the CSS).

WordPress.org

Pros:

No Advertising, Complete Control, You can host your own videos, access to thousands of plugins and themes to customize your site exactly how you want.

You own the blog (YOU.com), you can do with it however you see fit, and it looks more professional.

Cons:

You need your own server, domain name, and you have to install it (If you choose a host with Fantastico or 1 click install, installation is just a click away), you have to keep it up to date, and upgrade it on your own (checkout enlightenedwebmastery.com for a video tutorial on how to upgrade your WordPress installation).

Another con is sometimes you will have to deal with problems and errors, if you go wild installing a lot of things, you can break your installation and be offline for some time, no-one will be there to fix it, or prevent you from messing it up (like they would at WordPress.com)

Chapter 3 Summary

In this chapter we went over the differences between the various versions of WordPress as well as showed the pros and cons associated with choosing one of these options.

Chapter 3 Action Steps

Decide which version is right for you.

WordPress.org

If you'll be self hosting, you need to **buy a domain name**. I want you to spend some time thinking up ideas for your domain name.

If you are having problems coming up with a name, checkout **BustAname.com**. This site allows you to type in a few keywords and it provides possible options that you can use for your site

Next you need to choose a hosting provider.

DreamHost, HostGator, iMountain, and MediaTemple are all excellent options. GoDaddy also offers webhosting (shared-hosting) with a 1 click install option for WordPress. You can get started using GoDaddy for a couple of dollars a month.

WordPress.com

If you're going to use WordPress.com, I want you to spend 5 minutes and think up a name. This is very important and you need to know this before proceeding to the next chapter. Try and choose something that conveys your idea for your blog in as little words as possible.

If possible choose something sticky, something that once you hear it, you'll remember it (like Coca Cola).

Chapter 3 - Choosing which version of WordPress to use

Chapter 4

Getting started with WordPress.com

Introduction to chapter 4

In this chapter we will be going through the process of creating our site using WordPress.com. First we will create an account, then sign into that account. If you are going to be using WordPress.org, I recommend checking out chapter 22 first, to learn how to install WordPress (or if you're using a 1 click solution such as Fantastico) then come back and skim over the chapter and in chapter 5 we will be going over the dashboard.

Creating an account

To create an account, follow along with me, as I set up an account. Please remember you need to come up with your own user name. The name you want to use may not be available, if you are really stuck on using that name, something you can do is add numbers to the end, such as wordpress76.

Please note your username will be the same name as your hosted domain. The URL for your blog will be username.wordpress.com. So please take notice before you start your blog. Ilikepinkbunnies may be a good username, but if your blog deals with cooking, well.... that might be bad...

Chapter 4 - Getting started with WordPress.com

First off, go to *http://www.wordpress.com* and click the big button that says "Sign Up Now!".

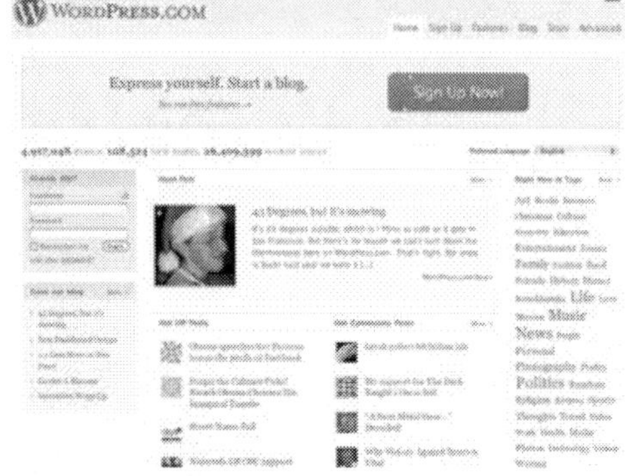

Next you need to type in a username, and give them a real email address. You also need to include some numbers in your password.

WordPress.com
Search WordPress.com Blogs
Go
Home
Sign Up
Features
Story
Advanced
Get your own WordPress.com account in seconds
Fill out this one-step form and you'll be blogging seconds later!
Username:
wpfoundations
(Must be at least 4 characters, letters and numbers only.)
Password:
Confirm:
Password Strength:
Good
Email Address:
wordpresstestaccount@gmail.com
(We send important administration notices to this address so triple-check it.)
Legal flotsam:
I have read and agree to the fascinating terms of service.
Gimme a blog! (Like username.wordpress.com)
Just a username, please.
Next »

When you are finished, click Next ->.

On this screen you're given the option to change your domain name, so it's different than your user name, and give your blog a title.

The language option is the language you will be typing in, if your typing will be in Spanish choose Spanish, otherwise leave it as English. This will not affect your menu items; you change that in a different section in the dashboard, which we will go over soon.

Your next choice is the following: "I would like my blog to appear in search engines like Google and Technorati, and in public listings around WordPress.com."

For almost EVERYTHING you do, you want this box checked, so others can find your website. As this is a test website, I am not clicking this button, but in real life, this is a button you would click.

When you are finished click the Signup button and continue on to the next page.

Type in your first and last name, along with some details about yourself. When you are finished click “save profile”.

Check your email, you should see an email from WordPress. Once that email arrives you need to open the email and click the link.

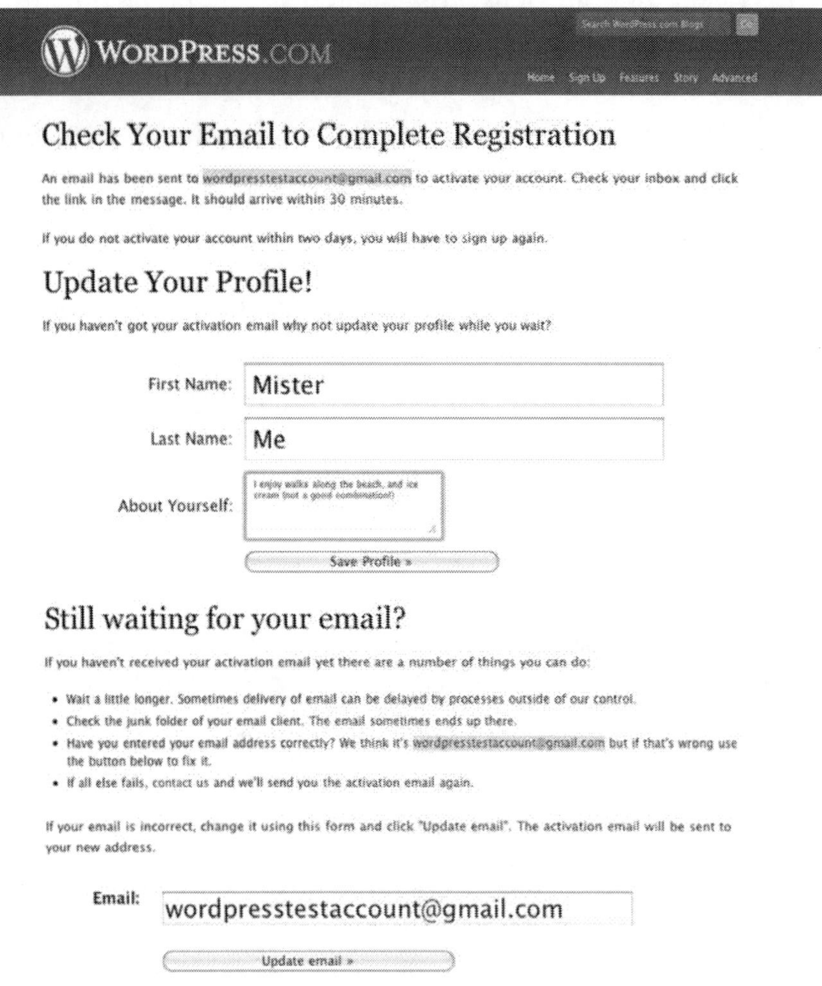

How to Log Into Your WordPress.com Account

Now that your account is ready, you can login to your blog, and take a look around the dashboard.

Please take note of this link, and post it in your bookmarks, as it will allow you instant access to your blog.

username.wordpress.com/wp-login.php

You need to replace username your account name (or domain name) on the previous screens. Self-hosted is u.com/wp-login.php

In my example, I would type in

wpfoundations for the username,

with *test1234* as password

Please note, if you click remember me, a cookie will get placed inside your browser, and whenever you visit this site on the same computer and browser, it will remember you. In other words, you don't want to do this on a public machine, or someone else's computer. The same applies when your browser asks if you want it to remember your password.

This is perfectly safe on your personal computer.

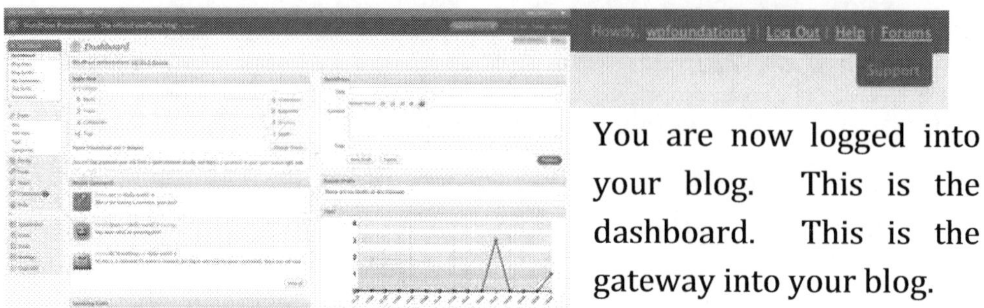

You are now logged into your blog. This is the dashboard. This is the gateway into your blog.

This is where you'll manage your blog.

To log out of your blog at any time, click the "Log Out" option at the top.

By default, when you create your blog, WordPress will apply a theme, throw in some widgets, and include a post on your blog. The blog title you gave earlier on will show up on the header graphic on your site.

To visit your site, while you are in dashboard, click the visit my site link, or type in *username.wordpress.com.*

http://wpfoundations.wordpress.com/

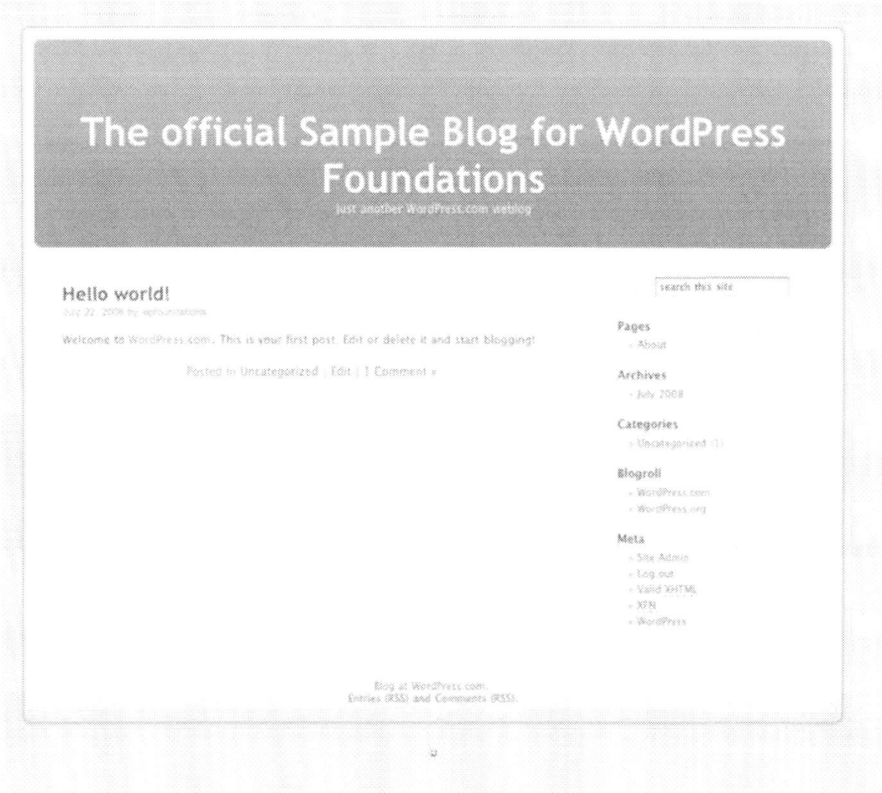

You can see a sample post, on the left. On the far right, you see a "sidebar", in it you have a search widget at the top, links to your "Pages", an "archives" widget, a "categories" widget, your "blog roll" widget, and the "meta widget", which allows you to do some administrative work on your site.

This is completely customizable, and we will get into how to edit it all later on in the book. (In chapters 9 and 10).

Chapter 4 Summary

In this chapter we walked through the process of creating an account on WordPress, activating the account and logging into that account.

We saw what our blog now looks like, and we are reading to start working on the blog.

Chapter 4 Action Steps

Sign up for an account at WordPress.com (if you're self hosting with WordPress.org, have WordPress.org installed and make sure you have successfully logged in).

Take note of your login page, login name and password.

Start thinking of how you would like your site to look.

A good idea is to go out and visit 5 sites that cover something similar to what you're going to be covering (news site, fan site, personal site, etc) and see what elements they have in common.

See what they have, that you like, that you want on your site.

Chapter 5

Getting started with Dashboard

Introduction to chapter 5

This is the chapter were we start to get our hands dirty. In this chapter you're going to tour the dashboard interface. You're going to become comfortable with it. Dashboard is the gateway to your blog. It is where you go to administer your site, add content, manage comments, see your stats and so much more.

New in 2.7

WordPress 2.7 has a new revamped dashboard interface. This can be both exciting and terrifying. The point behind the new interface is to avoid having to load up new screens just to access a certain menu. The goal is to have the most used parts accessible within 1-2 clicks.

Some of the other cool new features are, you can change how your dashboard looks when you login. You can move your panels around "modules" so you can have **stats** at the top right, **right now** (at a glance which lets you see if you got any new comments, how many posts you have, etc) on the left.

It's pretty nice to be able to position things how you see fit so if there is a feature you keep using, now you can keep it near the top so it's easily accessible. (please note, if your using .org you will need to install the WordPress stats plug-in to be able to use that module, I cover this on my website at enlightenedwebmastery.com under the post "**How To Install WordPress Plugins**".)

Another great feature is you can click "New Post" from the contextual menu located at the top of the dashboard interface.

QuickPress is a new feature that lets you start up a post right from your dashboard. You can give your post a title or write the body text, add images, movies and tags (no categories). You can click save draft, and come back and work on it later, or click "Publish" and it will be live on your site right away.

Recent Comments lets you not only see the most recent comments, but it also lets you moderate them directly from the dashboard module. Which is a very welcome and helpful feature.

Understanding the Interface

Here is a picture of what the main interface looks like:

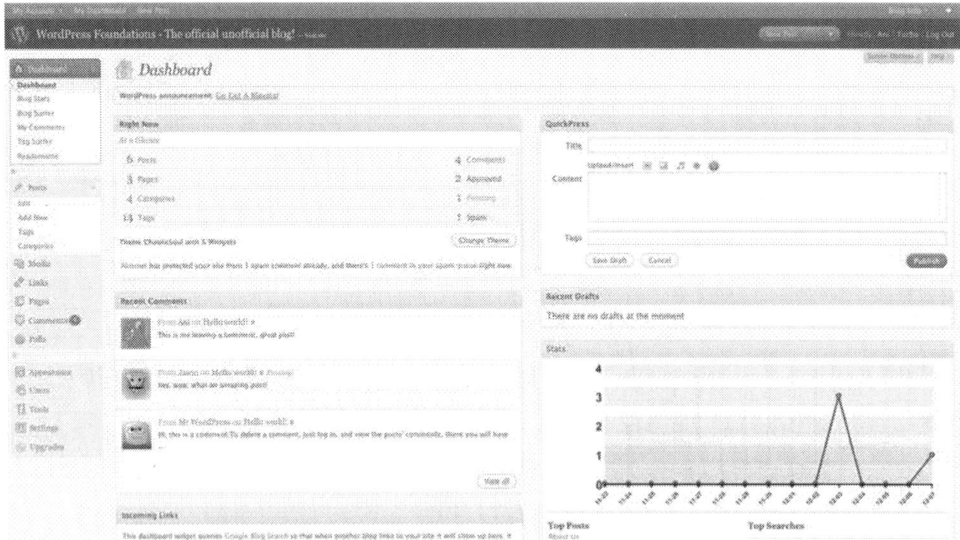

Clicking the title of the module (such as QuickPress) and dragging it around can move the “modules” into different positions, or you can minimize them by clicking the far right corner (an arrow will show up when you hover over it). You can also turn them off by using the screen options menu at the top.

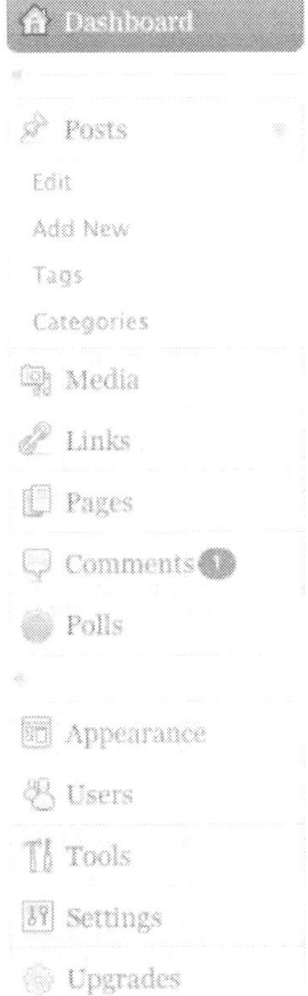

On the left side of your screen you will find the dashboard toolbox, it’s an “accordion style” menu system.

When you click one of the arrows on the far right hand side, the menu will slide down, and show you the options for that particular option.

If you click the name, you will be whisked away to that menu’s custom page, where you can set the options how you like. (Which was how it worked in previous editions of WordPress.)

Posts – This is the menu that allows you to choose to write a new post (Add New), manage your tags, manage your categories, or edit an already existing post. When you click "Posts" you're shown the same menu as if you clicked edit.

Media – This is the menu that allows you to manage your media library, or go ahead and upload a new file to your blog.

Links – This lets you add new links to your blog roll, edit already existing ones, or create categories for them. (i.e. friends, resources)

Pages – This lets you either edit or create a new page from scratch.

Comments – This tells you if you have any comments that need to be approved (notice the bright red 1), this menu does not drop down, but takes you right to the edit comments module (which you also can access on your main dashboard).

The next pane varies depending on if your using wordpress.com or wordpress.org.

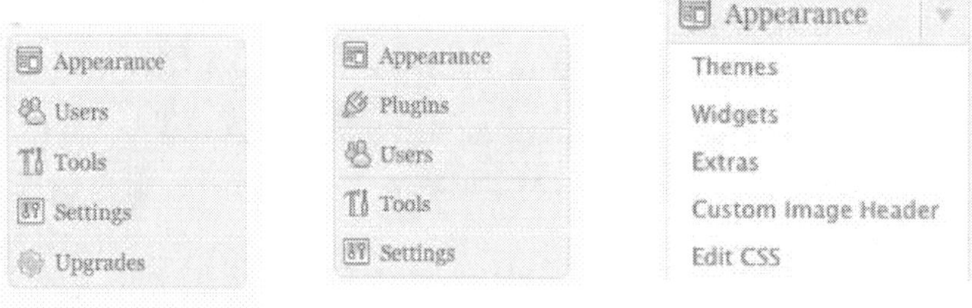

The difference is on WordPress.com you get Upgrades (which is a paid for feature) and on .org you can install Plugins.

Under the Appearance menu (shown on the previous page) for WordPress.com you have "Extras, Custom Image Header, and Edit CSS", these are WordPress.com specific features, and if you're self hosting you need not worry about them. (Chapters 11 and 12 cover these features).

Themes – By choosing themes you can change your theme on the fly. (WordPress.org includes Editor (where you can edit the individual php pages and code, and in some instances "Current Theme Options."

Widgets – These add additional functionality to your blog (search, calendar, and more), and is covered in chapter 10.

Edit CSS - is for WordPress.com users, it allows you to modify your CSS, and see how it looks. If you want to use this feature you need to pay some extra cash (learn more about extras in chapter 11).

If you are using a custom theme, or one you made yourself with extra functions, you may see additional options on your menu that lets you adjust theme specific features (such as special sliders)

Users - lets you add new users to your account, and manage who is there.

Tools – this is a new feature that I'm not going into here. But basically it lets you install "gears" (gears.google.com) which let's you speed up how pages load, and enable new features.

Settings – this is where you can adjust various settings for your blog, we will be covering this in the next chapter.

Plugins (.org only) this lets you see which plugins you have installed, activate new ones, edit them, or see custom plug-ins that have special options that you need to manage.

To learn more about plugins, check out the article and video I wrote on Enlightened WebMastery titled "**How To Install WordPress Plugins.**" On the website I show you several timesaving plugins that are beneficial depending on your situation, and usually include a video tutorial accompanied by text to ensure you get the most use out of the plugin.

enlightenedwebmastery.com/install-wordpress-plugins

Chances are if there is something you want to do with your blog, but cant quite figure out how, someone has likely wrote a plugin that automates the process for you.

Being able to install plugins should be reason enough to use WordPress.org to power your blog.

Due to the dynamic nature of plugins and the Internet, it wouldn't make much since to cover them in detail here in this book. So I encourage you to checkout the website for more information.

A Few New Modules

In this section I'm going to introduce you to the new modules available for WordPress inside the Dashboard.

These modules are available on both the .com and .org platforms.

Right Now - this is a fun new module. You can see at a glance your posts, how many comments you have, how many need approval, and more. This menu is also color-coded. Spam is red, pending is yellow, and approved comments are green.

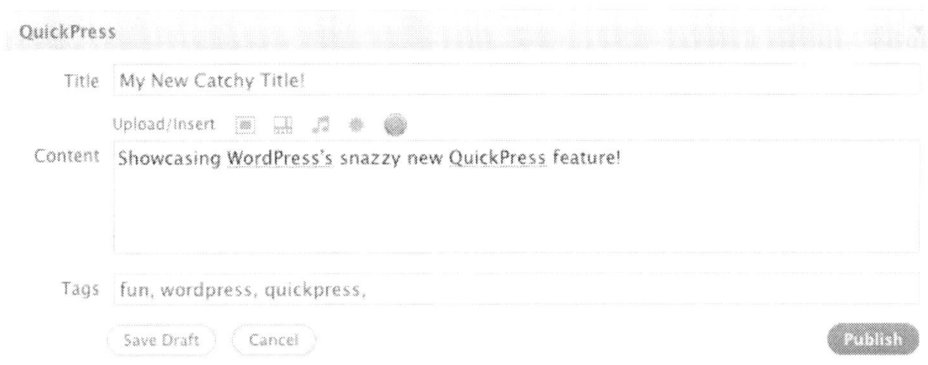

QuickPress – Inside this module you can write a new post. You can also save that post as a draft and access it later using the new Recent Drafts module.

Recent Drafts – This lets you see the latest drafts and be able to change them by clicking on them.

Recent Comments – from this interface, you can hover over each comment and approve, unapproved, reply, or mark it as spam. This is a very useful feature and a huge timesaver.

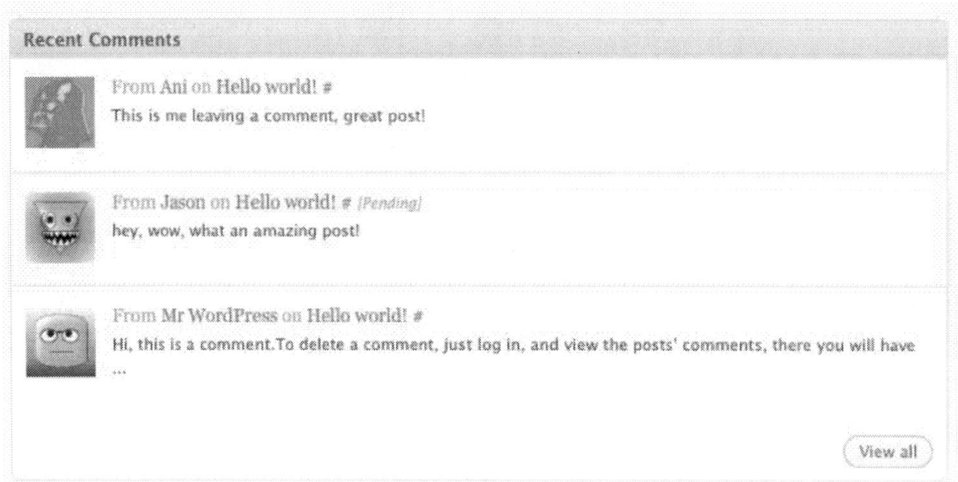

One last way to customize your interface is to click the "screen" option at the top of your dashboard. From here you can check or un-check certain modules to determine if they show up by default or not.

Chapter 5 Summary

In this chapter we toured the dashboard interface. You learned what's new in 2.7 and also learned about the functionally of the new modules.

I showed you how to customize your interface (by dragging the title bar of the modules and dragging them around) to enhance and speed up your workflow.

You learned how to navigate around the dashboard and learned how to use the toolbox on the left, and seen how easy it is to customize the dashboard.

Chapter 5 Action Steps

- Login to your site, checkout the dashboard and customize the interface to suit your needs.
- Learn how to navigate the dashboard and get a good "feel" for where things are and the logical structure behind the design.
- This is where you will be spending most of your time, so feel free to take the time necessary to take it in and get the most out of your dashboard.

Chapter 5 - Getting started with Dashboard

Chapter 6

Setting up your blog

Introduction to chapter 6

This is a rather long chapter. Any time you setup a blog, you should keep this chapter open as a reference, as it walks you through the steps.

Due to the length, and rather dry nature of this chapter, I encourage you to just follow along with me as I explain each part of the interface so you don't need to read it again.

Make sure you take notes of anything of particular importance to you so that later on whenever your setting up a new blog, it will take you less time.

Please note if you're using the WordPress.org platform, you cannot create a Gravatar from within the WordPress interface, and instead you need to visit gravatar.com and sign up for an account, and post up your picture.

You still need to enable Gravatar support for your blog.

The benefit of setting up a Gravatar account is so that whenever you post a comment on another website and enter your email address your picture will show up next to your post automatically.

I recommend signing up and creating a Gravatar account even if you're using WordPress.com, as your WordPress.com avatar does not carry over to other blogs (unless you're using the same email address).

Editing Your Profile

Before we get started making content, we need to set some options on your user profile, and perform some tasks.

The quickest way to get there, is to click your name at the top of the dashboard, you will then see the following:

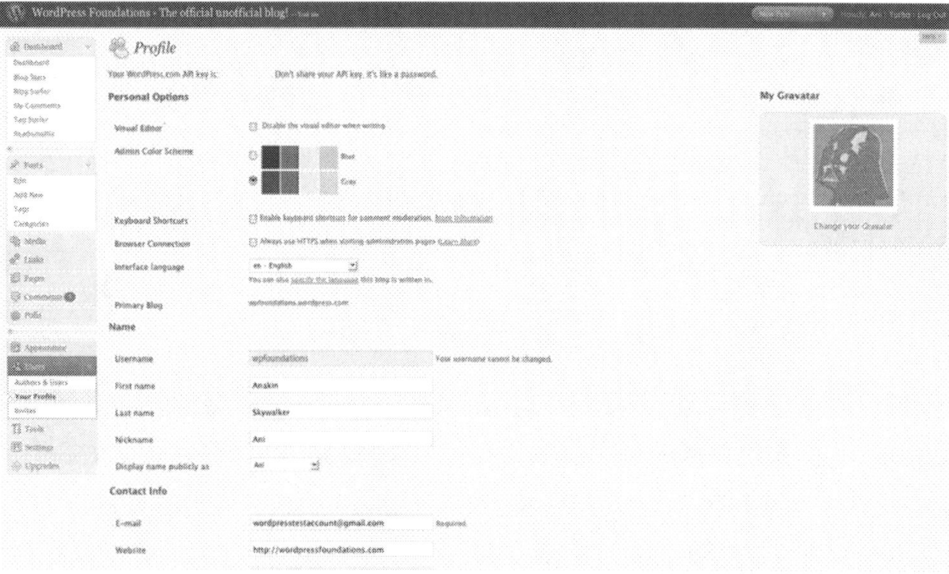

Editing Your Profile and Personal Options

Personal Options

Visual Editor — Disable the visual editor when writing

Admin Color Scheme — Blue / Gray

Keyboard Shortcuts — Enable keyboard shortcuts for comment moderation. More information

Browser Connection — Always use HTTPS when visiting administration pages (Learn More)

Interface language — en - English

You can also specify the language this blog is written in.

Primary Blog — wpfoundations.wordpress.com

The visual editor allows you instant access to high end formatting options, such as bolding, setting header information, as well as allowing other various formatting options right from the interface itself. I highly recommend keeping this enabled.

The color scheme is how the admin panel looks.

The interface language is what the interface language is. If you're not a native English reader, you might want to change the option to your language of choice to better navigate the interface.

Primary Blog is the link to your main blog on wordpress.com, if you have another blog on wordpress.com you can change whichever you want to be your primary.

To the right of this screen, you get the option of uploading your picture. This can be you, or an "avatar" image. Click Choose File, and select one from your hard drive, then click Upload Image.

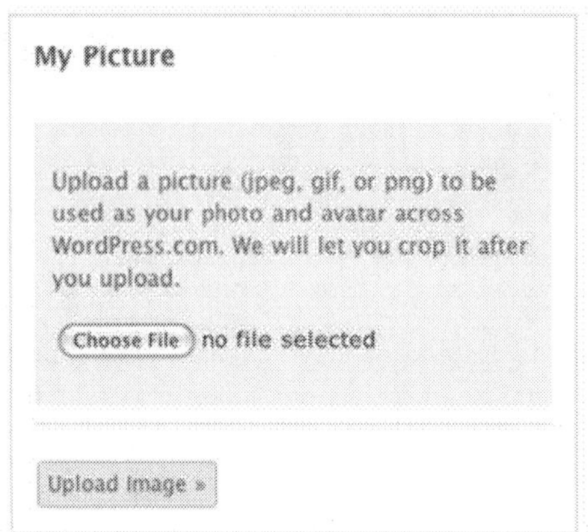

Your image needs to be around 128x128, so after you upload this image, you will need to "crop the image" which means making it fit into those boundaries.

You will be whisked away to a screen similar to this:

The square with "marching ants" is your 128x128 boundary. If you want to resize, only click on the corner boundaries, as I did here.

When you are happy with your selection, click crop, and you will be taken to the next page.

Your new avatar will show up now, both on your blog, and on wordpress.com. Whenever you leave a comment on another WordPress.com website, they will see your avatar.

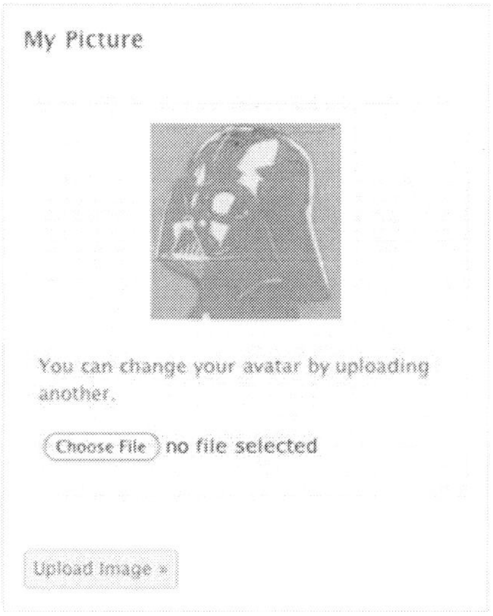

All done!

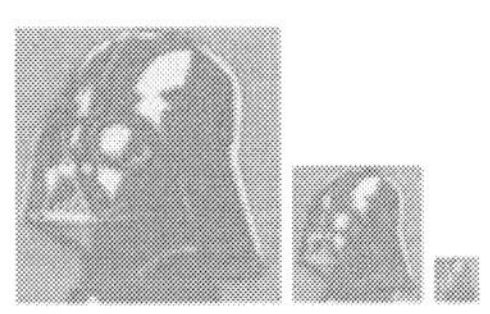

Your avatar image has been uploaded and you should start seeing it appear around WordPress.com soon!

Updating Your Name and Personal Details

Name

Username	wpfoundations	Your username cannot be changed
First name	Anakin	
Last name	Skywalker	
Nickname	Ani	
Display name publicly as	wpfoundations	

You cannot change your username. Input a First name, and a Last name. Then proceed with a Nickname.

Whenever you hit "Update" at the bottom, you will then be able to change your online name via a drop down box.

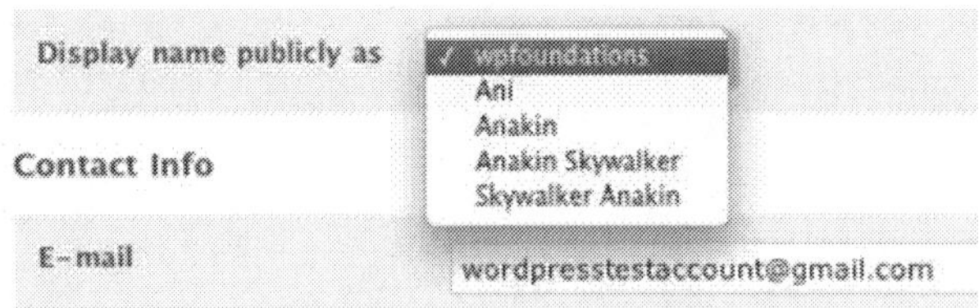

If you wish to change your main email at any point, please do so here. Insert any website you wish to be displayed under your profile here (you can list a website other than the wordpress.com url, as I did here).

AIM is your AOL instant messenger nick, same with yahoo, and Google. These are entirely optional.

Contact Info

E-mail	wordpresstestaccount@gmail.com	Required
Website	wordpressfoundations.com	
AIM		
Yahoo IM		
Jabber / Google Talk		

Now you can insert some information about you and your hobbies.

About Yourself

Biographical Info

When I'm not running The Galactic Empire, I like to blog about my evil doings on wordpress.com.

Share a little biographical information to fill out your profile. This may be shown publicly.

After that, we need to change your password to something more secure. Try adding numbers, uppercase letters, and symbols. You need to remember this, so don't make it hard on yourself, you just don't want people stealing your account. A good example password is - w0rdPre$$.

When you are done, click the Update Profile button below, and then click “Settings” at the top.

When you are done, click the Update Profile button below, then click the settings tab on the left, and choose “General”.

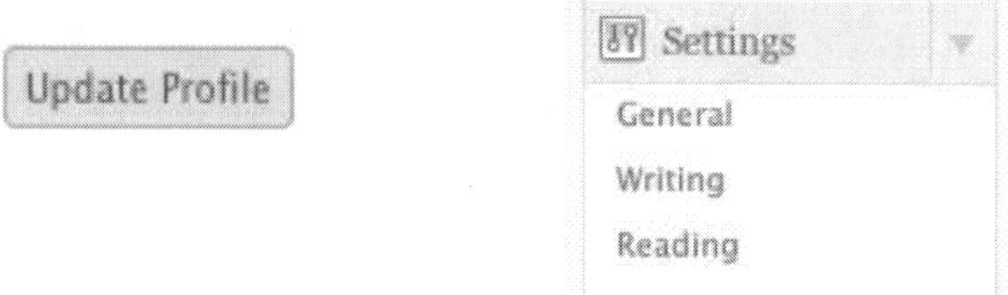

Now we need to work on updating the settings on the blog, and making it more personal for us.

Configuring The Settings For Your Blog.

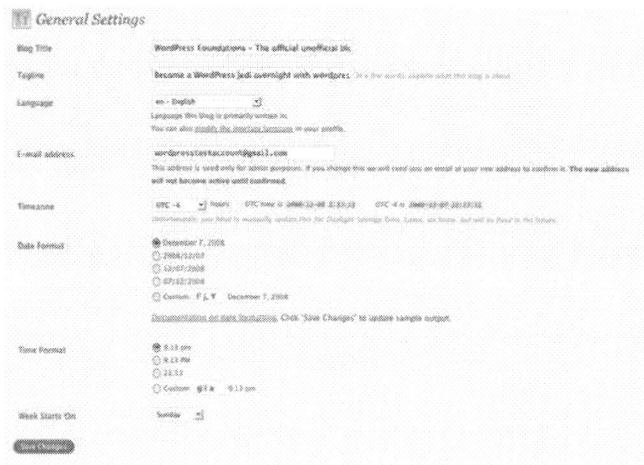

The Blog Title will appear on the "Header" of your blog, which is located at the top.

The Tagline is what is listed below your Header.

Language tells wordpress.com what language you're writing in.

Email is your current email address.

Membership, is if you want people to create accounts on your website before they can comment, it's up to you if you want to do this or not. I don't because when I go to someone's blog, and have to sign up, I usually won't comment.

Time zone. Look at the UTC time, see what it is, and the difference between UTC and your time. Then select that option.

You can change the **Date and Time format** if you want; I like this default setting, as it works for us in the US.

Here you can choose what day of the week is the start for you. In the US it is Sunday. The default is Monday.

Be sure to hit the **"Save Changes"** button at the bottom.

Then click on the "writing" option under Settings on the left (under General).

Changing The Writing and Reading Settings on Your Blog

Writing Settings

Size of the post box	20 lines
Formatting	☑ Convert emoticons like :-) and :-P to graphics on display ☐ WordPress should correct invalidly nested XHTML automatically
Default Post Category	Random
Default Link Category	Blogroll

Size of the post box - how big your editor box is.

Formatting - changes smiles into graphical smiles.

Default Post Category - the default category for your posts. If you write mainly news, choose news. (Note you need to create categories before they will show up here, we cover category creation in Chapter 17.) I highly recommend setting up a "blog" category or news category and set that as your default category opposed to leaving the default "uncategorized".

Default Link Category - Change your default Link categories.

Save Changes, and Click Reading.

Reading Settings

Front page displays
Your latest posts
A static page (select below)
- Front page: - Select -
- Posts page: - Select -

Blog pages show at most 10 posts

Syndication feeds show the most recent 10 posts

For each article in a feed, show
Full text
Summary

For each article in an enhanced feed, show
Categories
Tags
Comment count
Add to Stumbleupon
Add to Del.icio.us
Add to Digg.com
Add to Reddit
Changes may not appear until you create a new post or your news reader refreshes.

Encoding for pages and feeds
UTF-8
The character encoding you write your blog in (UTF-8 is recommended)

Front-page displays - choose if you want a certain page to always be on your home page.

Blog pages show at most - How many posts to show at most. When you have more, it will show a previous or next.

Syndication feeds show the most recent - How many feeds show up when someone subscribes to your RSS Feed (I bump this to 12-15 normally).

For each article in a feed, show – choose if you want people who subscribe via RSS to get the full post, or just a summary.

For each article in an enhanced feed, show - For those readers, what do you want to show up in your feed.

Encoding for pages and feeds - Leave the encoding alone, it is what you need, unless you need something else, and if you do, you will know.

Click "Save Changes"

Setting the Discussion Options for your Blog

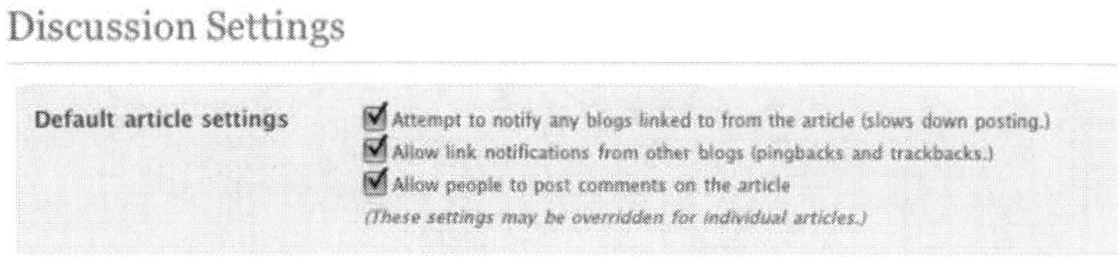

Discussion Settings

Default article settings

Attempt to notify any blogs linked to from the article (slows down posting.)
Allow link notifications from other blogs (pingbacks and trackbacks.)
Allow people to post comments on the article
(These settings may be overridden for individual articles.)

The first option means while you are posting something to your blog, and commenting about another blog, it will automatically send a trackback to that article on the other person's blog.

The second option is whenever someone else writes a post about something you posted and links to it, they will ping back your article, and it will appear under the comments on your blog.

The last option is if you want to allow others the ability to leave comments on the article. I highly recommend this, as I see no point in having a blog without comments.

You can have WordPress automatically email you whenever someone makes a post on your blog, or when a comment is being held for moderation.

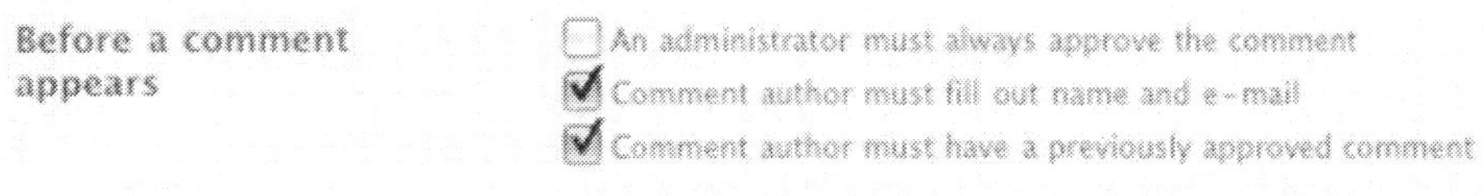

If you check the first option, you will have to approve every post. If you are really worried about spam, this can be a great idea to have checked. You will need to check your comments constantly to keep approving them, and this can become real tedious if your site becomes popular.

The second option means when someone posts, they have to enter their name and email.

Third means if you set it up so you have to approve everything, if this user has already been approved, he can go ahead and post without needing clearance.

Comment Moderation

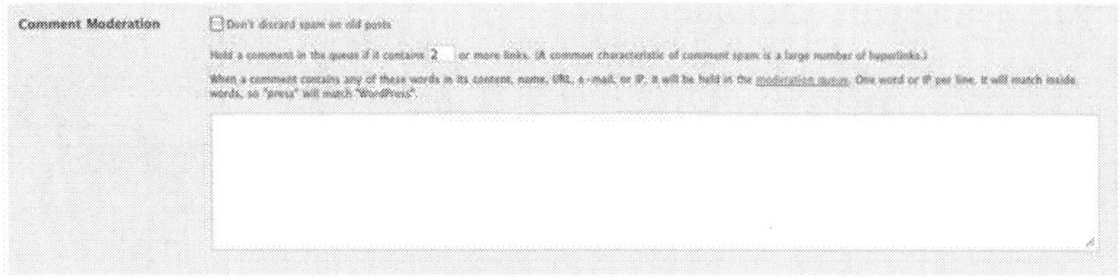

Hold a comment in the queue if it contains a certain number or more links. (A common characteristic of comment spam is a large number of hyperlinks.) This can be a good way to stop spam, I keep it at 2, which is fine for the most part, because someone might be replying to my post and posting a link to help.

Some people really do post valid links, sometimes multiple links; it pays to check your comments, as you could be getting real posts that are not spam.

When a comment contains any of these words in its content: name, URL, e-mail, or IP, it will be held in the moderation queue. One word or IP per line. It will match inside words, so "press" will match "WordPress".

If you don't want certain topics being posted, you can fix it so these kinds of posts do not show up. Such as "Religion", "Politics", "Sex" or anything else you don't want talked about in the comments of your blog.

If you put the words as Blacklist, the comment will automatically be marked as spam, and you have a chance to review it, but in 15 days it is GONE.

Enabling Avatars on Your Blog

An avatar is an image-based representation of you. We set up one earlier when we setup the profile for this account. People associate you with your avatar, if you use the same one on multiple forums; it helps people keep track of you. If you used my avatar I setup here for an example, people would remember you as the pink Vader, regardless of your username.

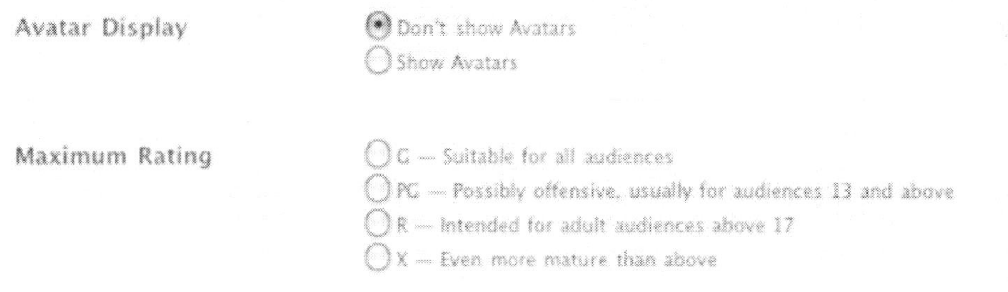

You have the option of allowing this or not. I would, as they are fun to look at, and add personality.

You can setup a rating, so inappropriate avatars do not show up on your site.

If your running your local church's website, you might not want people commenting with naked people or curse words on their images. I think PG is a good setting to choose, it's not too restrictive.

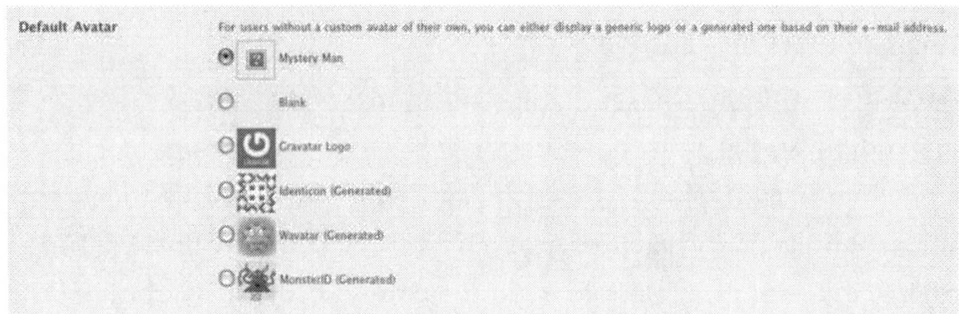

The next thing you can do is select a default Avatar.

The first is the "Mystery Man" which you cannot see here, but is just a gray picture of a man.

Blank is Blank.

Gravatar is the logo for that company.

The next 3 are randomly generated, each user will have a different avatar, and will be unique to them, and thus, not inappropriate in the least.

Click "save" and move on to Privacy Settings.

Adjusting The Privacy Settings of Your Blog.

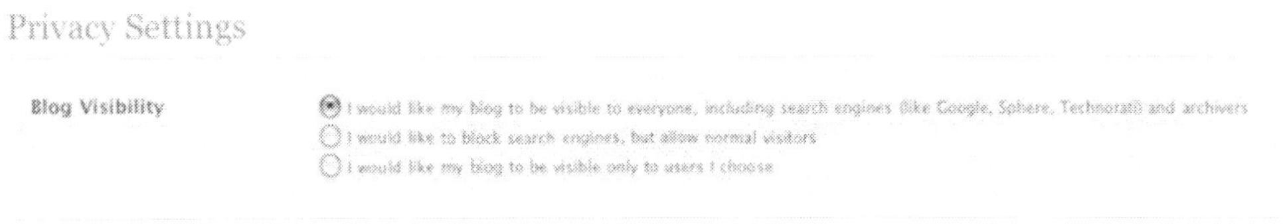

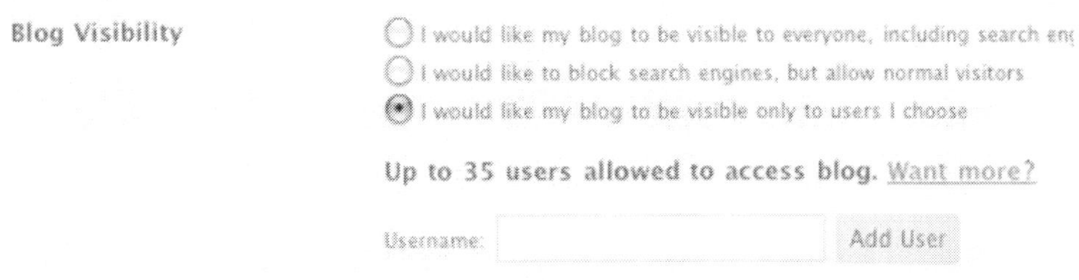

Privacy Settings

Blog Visibility

I would like my blog to be visible to everyone, including search engines (like Google, Sphere, Technorati) and archivers
I would like to block search engines, but allow normal visitors
I would like my blog to be visible only to users I choose

Blog Visibility

I would like my blog to be visible to everyone, including search en
I would like to block search engines, but allow normal visitors
I would like my blog to be visible only to users I choose

Up to 35 users allowed to access blog. Want more?

Username: Add User

(1) *I would like my blog to be visible to everyone, including search engines (like Google, Sphere, and Technorati) and archive's.*

This is the option you need to select if you want your blog indexed (and you usually do)

(2) *I would like to block search engines, but allow normal visitors.*

This means anyone can visit your blog, they just need to know the address.

(3) *I would like my blog to be visible only to users I choose.*

This means you need to send out invites, and the user needs to have a wordpress.com account. You can only have 35 users, so choose this option quite wisely.

Click Save Changes.

Delete Blog, deletes your blog! Media lets you choose the dimensions of the images that are displayed on your blog. OpenID is a special feature that let's you login to OpenID based sites using your login here.

Domains, is a paid feature for WordPress.com users. It costs 10 dollars per year. It allows you.com to point to you.wordpress.com.

Chapter 6 Summary

You made it! I know this was a pretty long and grueling chapter, I hope you didn't fall asleep, and I promise there are no more chapters like this in the book.

In this chapter we went over the entire process of setting up the options for your blog.

You created an avatar (and hopefully a Gravatar) and setup your blog to your specifications.

Now that you have your blog setup and ready to go, it's time to get blogging. In the next chapter we will start writing posts.

Chapter 6 Action Steps

After reading this chapter you should have completed the following: (if not, you really need to before you move onto another chapter)

- Setup your profile
- Created an avatar for your WordPress.com account
- Created a Gravatar for yourself (that way when you post on a wordpress.org blog or someone else's blog, people can see that it's you.)
- Setup your personal information
- Configured the settings for your blog
- Changed the discussion settings for your blog.

This chapter concludes the initial setup phase for your blog. Anytime you setup a new blog, you will need to go through tear through this chapter.

If you didn't set up some parts of your blog right now, that's ok. Sometimes you will not know what you want, until you know what you want. After you have your blog setup, you have some posts, some comments, and you're used to the interface, it may be a good idea to recheck your settings and modify them as necessary.

Chapter 6 - Setting up your blog

Chapter 7

Writing Posts

Introduction to chapter 7

This is the chapter were we learn how to start writing posts. This is a very detailed chapter and quite long. You don't need to memorize it, if you are confused that is perfectly ok.

This chapter goes over the writing interface and explains exactly how to take full advantage of the writing panel.

I recommend that you follow along with this chapter with your blog, and take note of anything of importance. I recommend highlighting important parts of this chapter as well as placing post-it flags where you see the most value.

Besides just covering the writing panel, I also go over some very important tagging and category strategies. This is some very high level stuff, so I recommend paying strict attention to them.

I have included a reference list of keyboard shortcuts that you can use when writing a post inside WordPress. Not all of them will be immediately useful, and I encourage you to not try and memorize them all. Just look at them, and notice if any shortcut seems valuable to you. If it does, write it down, mark it, and try and remember it.

You don't need to memorize any shortcuts, so please don't get too hung up on them. If you find it useful, implement it, if not, feel free to skip that whole section.

Accessing the Writing Panel

At the top of your wordpress.com dashboard (top right), click "new post" and you will see something similar to the following.

Writing Your First Post

While you are in this panel, we may as well go over how to write a post on your blog. This is where you'll spend most of your time when working on your blog, so lets go over how to use it. I will discuss this from the top down. Starting with the Title, which is what you see at top.

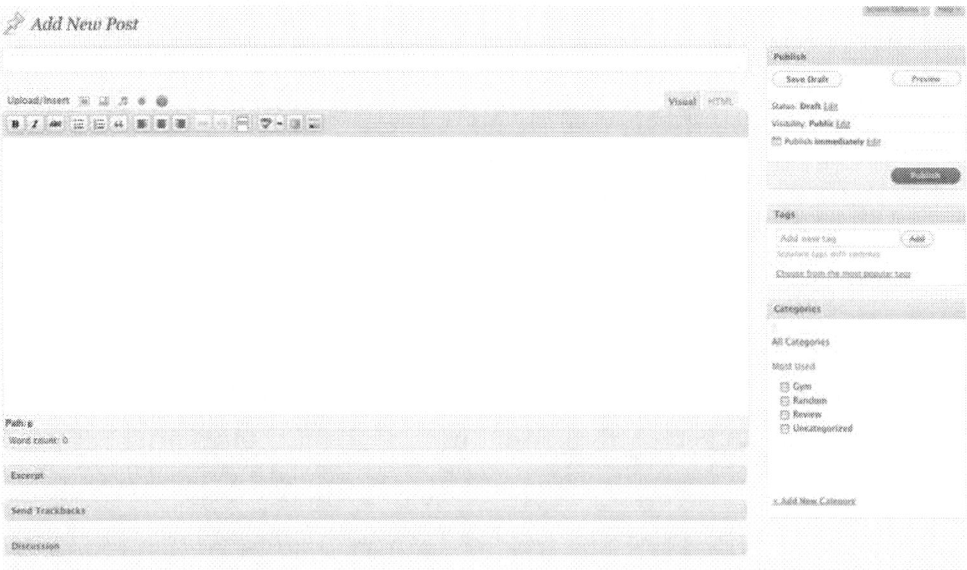

At the top under "Add New Post" is where you put the **title.** From here you type in the title for your post. This title will make up part of your permalink and will show up inside the address bar of your readers browser.

Next is the **menu bar**, if you click the last button, it opens up everything, including the kitchen sink. This is where you select if you want to bold items, make lists, create quotes, or spell check.

Below that is where you **write** your actual post.

The box underneath is where you write a brief **excerpt**. This is a very important habit to form as it keeps you from adding duplicate content to your site. This will show up in your archives, if you leave this blank, the first few words of your post will show up.

Next is **Send Trackbacks** which you do not need to modify (usually) as wordpress automatically sends out trackbacks.

Below that is the **Discussion** panel here is where you choose if you want to enable comments or not.

To the right of this window, is another panel.

The top panel is called **Publish** – clicking this button publishes your post for the world to see. (You can also save it as a draft)

Below that is where you add **tags**. Tags are similar but different than categories. They are discussed later on in this chapter.

Below that is the **category** panel, from here you select a category for your post.

Here is what your page might look like after you type in some content:

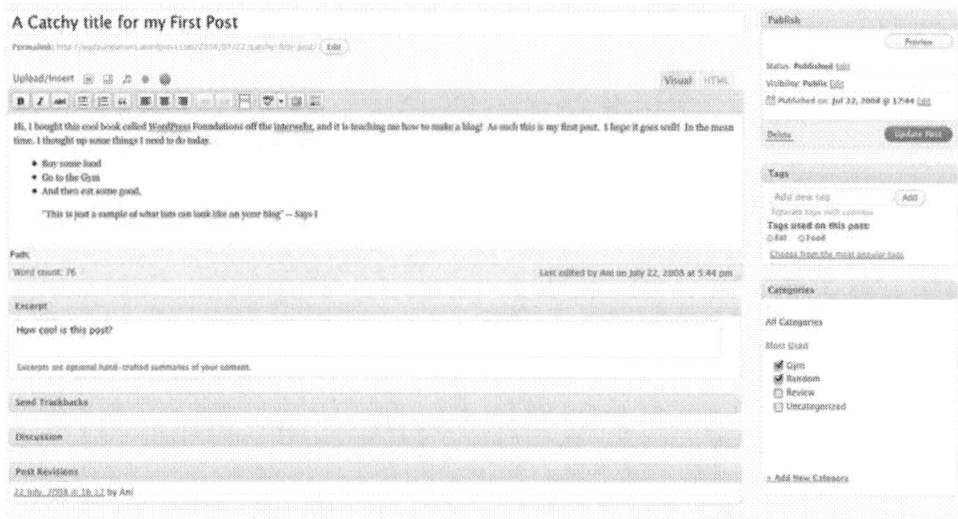

I created a post with a list and a quote, and added in some tags along with a category.

We have a problem here, check out the link below.

wpfoundations.wordpress.com/2009/01/22/a-catchy-title...end/

This is not the kind of link you want on your blog. It is far to long. You need to change it. Click the edit button, and change it to something shorter as below.

wpfoundations.wordpress.com/2009/01/22/a-catchy-title/

This is a much simpler URL, and will be easier to remember. Please check your permalink before you publish any article to ensure that you have a URL that you like.

The fine art of tagging

Tags are a recent addition to WordPress. Tags provide a quick and easy way to tag your work. For example, you can write a post on news (maybe you're writing a political piece on president Obama), you can tag the article as Obama (opposed to dedicating a whole category to him). By using more and more tags, you create a way for your readers to find similar posts.

When you create tags, you need to try and stay consistent.

Develop a scheme. Obama, obama, obama-news or Obama_News.

Categories

Categories are different from tags. I link to think of it in the following way: Categories = General, Tag = Specific.

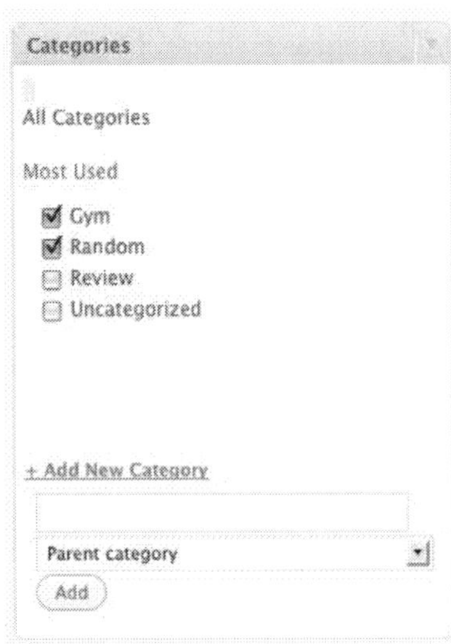

It's a good practice to keep your categories to a minimum, and use tags to their full advantage. This way you can keep your categories very focused.

If you had a video game blog and made a category for every game that came out, you would soon have far to many categories to manage or to be of any real use.

A better plan would be as follows. Create categories called Xbox 360, PS3, and Wii.

And instead of making categories for each game, you create tags for each game.

The obvious benefit here is, when a new game comes out for a new platform (Xbox 360), you can write about the game (under the category Xbox 360) and "tag" the game as GTA 4.

When a user comes to your site via Google, they can then click on that tag to read more on that game, or the category to read about more games for that platform. This example works regardless if you are doing a blog on games or not. You can categorize music, news, movies, etc. I highly recommend keeping your categories to a minimum, and use tags as much as possible.

Let's go over the different formatting options available while using the visual editor.

Starting from the top left, lets discuss each of these in detail:

B - This Bolds your text.
I - This provides italics.
ABC - is the strike through option, so you can write ~~stupid~~ smart text and write over it.

The next two buttons create lists, the first one uses bullets, and the second creates numbered lists.

The next button creates a block quote, which is useful when you are quoting and want things to stand out.

The next three buttons determine the alignment of your text, if you want it left aligned, centered, or right aligned choose the appropriate button.

The next option deals with creating hyper links (these are words you can click to visit a different website).

The first button creates a link, to do this, highlight the

text you wish to make a link and click that button.

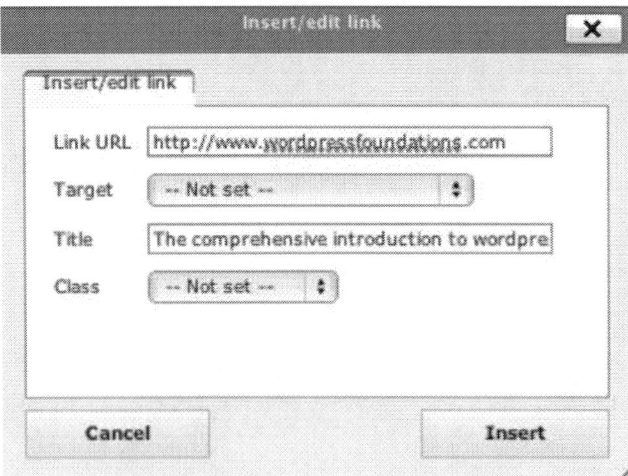

Type in the URL, including http://

The target is if you want the link to open up in a new window or the same window. (leaving the option at Not set bases the behavior off the users default browser behavior)

Title is what will appear when someone hovers over your link (the ALT text)

Class deals with custom CSS code.

The next button inserts a more tag, which lets you write an introductory paragraph, and have only that show up on your front page, it will create a "click here to read more" message, and when they click, they will see the whole post (on a new page).

The next button is your spellchecker. Which helps you check your words for spelling errors.

The next button makes this screen take up your full screen, thus giving you more space to write with.

The last button either shows or hides the kitchen sink.

These are the buttons you see when you show the kitchen sink.

The format drop down menu, lets you select some text, and change how it is formatted.

This lets you choose between paragraph text, as well as your header tags such as h1, h2 and h3.

The next option underlines your text, please be careful with this, as when most people see underlined text they think it is a link.

The next button aligns your text as “full” or justified.

The A will change the color of your text, again be careful with this, as most links are a different color and your user may interpret inline text that is a different color to be a link.

The next 2 buttons are for pasting in text from other programs. The first one is from a plain text editor, and the second is for Microsoft Word. It gets rid of all the non-standard editing Word applies to text.

The Eraser will get rid of custom formatting.

The Omega symbol allows you to insert symbols into your blog.

The next two are your undo, and redo's, (does the same thing as cmd z or control z does in your normal programs) allowing you to undo some changes you just made.

The last button is help; click it when you need some additional help.

Learn and Master The Visual Editors Shortcuts

Learning this shortcuts can save you time. If you find when you're writing posts you're constantly using a certain function (such as copy, paste, bold or spell check, it may be worth the time to learn those specific shortcuts. If you're using a Macintosh use **Command + Letter**, if you're using Linux, or Windows, use **Ctrl + letter**.

Action	Letter
Copy	c
Paste	v
Select all	a
Cut	x
Undo	z
Redo	y

These shortcuts require using Alt (option) + Shift + letter.

Action	Letter
Bold	b
Italic	i
Check Spelling	n
Align Left	l
Justify Text	j
Align Center	c
~~Strikethrough~~	d
Align Right	r
List	u
Insert link	a
1. List	o
Remove link	s
Quote	q
Insert Image	m
Full Screen	g
Insert More Tag	t
Insert Page Break tag	p
Help	h
Switch to HTML mode	e

The HTML Editor

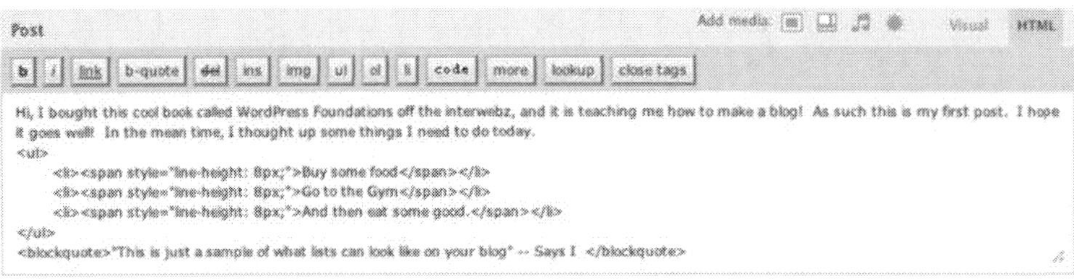

If you prefer to write your posts in pure HTML, then you should checkout the HTML editor. To access it, just click the HTML button.

The editor comes with buttons you can press to insert code that works with WordPress. Most people rarely add HTML to a post, and tend to stick with using the Visual Editor. The main reason I use HTML on a WordPress blog, is to add in code, and functionality.

I have noticed a bug that whenever I'm in HTML mode, and have some <SCRIPT> code, or <IFRAME> code it disappears when I go back and forth from visual to HTML, so please save often, and copy (CTRL + A or CMD + A Then CTRL + C Then CTRL + V to paste) your HTML post before you switch back to visual (if your going between them) to avoid heartache incase something "disappears", this always happens to me when adding Amazon widgets to a post.

Publishing Your Post

Now that you have a post ready, and you know the basics of the editor, the next step is to click publish (at the top right of your post, near the title). This will publish your post to your blog.

When you do this, make sure you click "Visit Site" at the top of your dashboard to see how it looks!

Viewing Your First Post

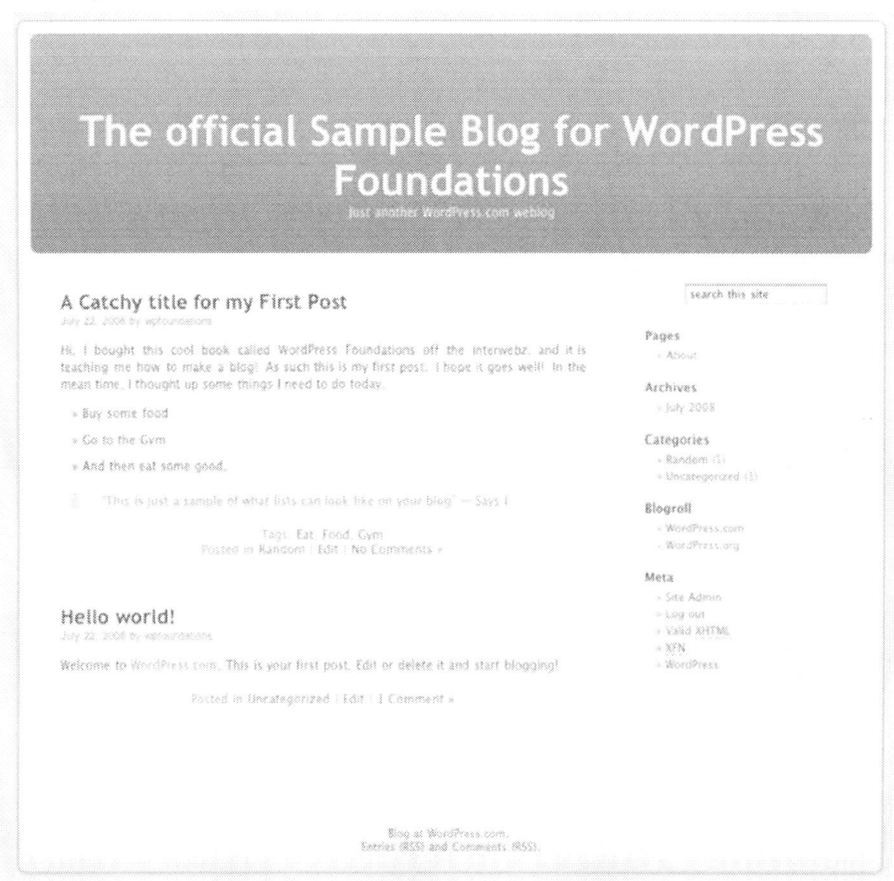

The new post is posted at the top of the page. Every time you make a post, it is filed in reverse-chronological order. Meaning the newest post is always at the top.

Chapter 7 Summary

This chapter covered the writing panel in detail. You know how exactly what each button does, and you know some shortcuts.

You were introduced to Tags and Categories (remember when using tags to think specific (Obama, Halo, Fried Beans) and when using categories think general (Politics, Xbox 360, Recipes).

You learned how to use the HTML editor, and some potential things to look out for.

Chapter 7 Action Steps

Before moving onto the next chapter, complete the following tasks:

- Write a sample post
- Create a post with a list, some bullets and a quote
- Emphasize some words by using the B I and U options

Next I want you to get out a piece of paper and spend 5-10 minutes on the following exercise:

Ask yourself what your blog is about, what it's going to cover. Think up some categories and tags that you can use.

Remember Specific = Tag, General = Category

Once you have a list, keep it near, we will be inputting them in chapter 17.

Chapter 8

Creating pages

Introduction to chapter 8

In this chapter you will learn about pages, how to manage them, and the difference between a page and a post.

One thing to consider when creating your website (especially if you're going to use Googles PPC (Ad Words)) is creating a Privacy Policy, Terms of Condition, Contact Us, and an About Us page to avoid getting "The Google Slap".

If Google visit's your site (they will) and they don't like what they see they can and will "Slap" you. What this means is your PPC Ad Campaigns jump way up. You could be paying 50 cents a click today, then get slapped, and pay 5$ the next day.

So if you are collecting any information, be sure to have the above mentioned items on your website.

How pages differ from posts.

Pages are typically not frequently updated, an exception to that would be if you ran a restaurant and wanted to showcase specials. Since this is important to your site, you need to create a dedicated page for this material. When you have this page, you can give it to anyone, they can then visit your website, view that page and see the specials. Since you will not be showing older specials, you can change it anytime, and no one will ever see the older content.

Pages are more static compared to your "main content" and as such; you will not be updating pages as often, so it's a good idea to turn off commenting on these pages. We'll go over how to do that shortly.

Writing Your First Page

On your dashboard, click on the Pages menu on the left hand side, and click "Add New".

This layout is very similar as when you are writing a post, though there are some exceptions.

Give the page a Title "About Us" and type in some sample information that you want people to see when clicking the "About Us" page on your blog.

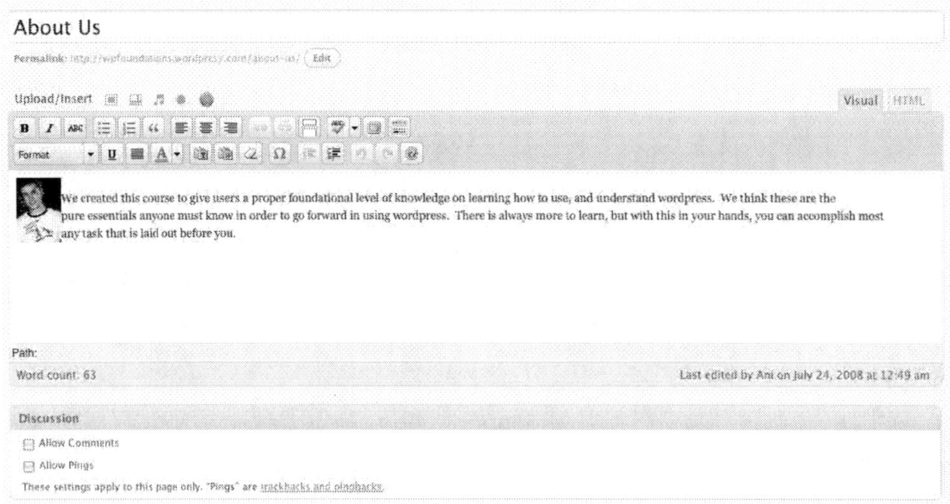
About Us
Edit
Upload/Insert
Visual
HTML
Format
We created this course to give users a proper foundational level of knowledge on learning how to use, and understand wordpress. We think these are the pure essentials anyone must know in order to go forward in using wordpress. There is always more to learn, but with this in your hands, you can accomplish most any task that is laid out before you.
Path:
Word count: 63
Last edited by Ani on July 24, 2008 at 12:49 am
Discussion
Allow Comments
Allow Pings
These settings apply to this page only. "Pings" are trackbacks and pingbacks.

I highly recommend deselecting Allow Comments, and Allow Pings, which you will find under the discussions section, then click update. (Unless the page is a resource page of some kind, then leave it checked, so people can comment and link to it.)

Now that you have your page written, and those two options deselected, click Publish (same location as before) then click Visit Site, to view your page.

Pages
» About
» About Us

You will see the new Page you just made, we just made About Us, go ahead and click it.

The URL for that page and others you make will be similar to the following - *http://wpfoundations.wordpress.com/about-us/.*

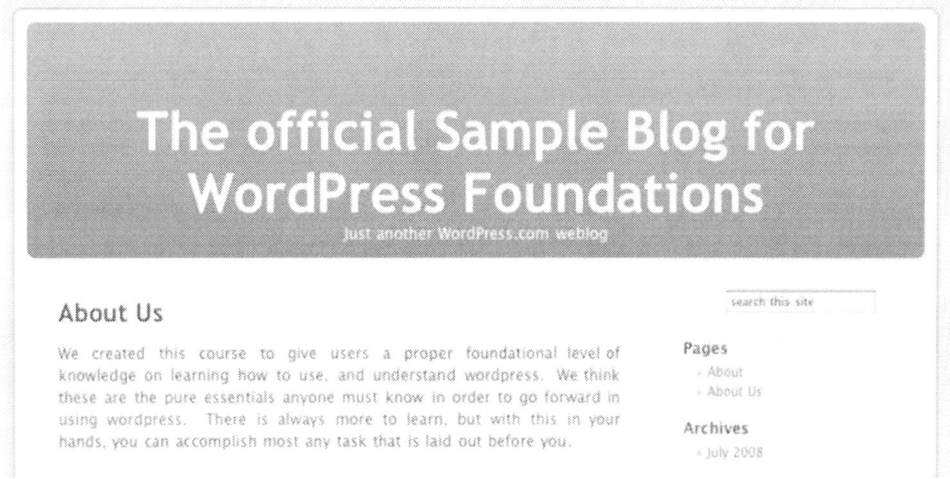
The official Sample Blog for WordPress Foundations
Just another WordPress.com weblog
About Us
We created this course to give users a proper foundational level of knowledge on learning how to use, and understand wordpress. We think these are the pure essentials anyone must know in order to go forward in using wordpress. There is always more to learn, but with this in your hands, you can accomplish most any task that is laid out before you.
search this site
Pages
About
About Us
Archives
July 2008

Next we need to cover another task, which is dependent on your theme. Go ahead and make a new Page and follow along.

We'll be using a feature called **Templates** so create a new page, and give it the name, "View our Archives".

Leave the Page blank, as you do not need to type anything.

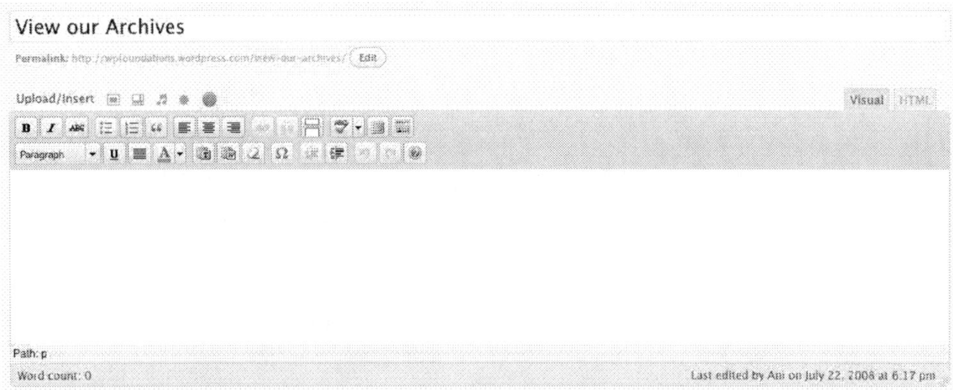

In the Attributes Panel to the right, change the template, to archives. When you're finished click Publish.

Attributes

Parent

Main Page (no parent)

You can arrange your pages in hierarchies, for example you could have an "About" page that has "Life Story" and "My Dog" pages under it. There are no limits to how deeply nested you can make pages.

Template

Archives

Some themes have custom templates you can use for certain pages that might have additional features or custom layouts. If so, you'll see them above.

Order

0

Pages are usually ordered alphabetically, but you can put a number above to change the order pages appear in. (We know this is a little janky, it'll be better in future releases.)

If you do not see this option, it is because your "theme" does not support this template. I'm using the default theme (Kubrick).

What this did, was allow WordPress to dynamically create a page for us, that links to the archives on our site. This is a great feature, and some themes support **Page Templates** while others offer none.

This is why I warned you, if you change to another theme (which we'll cover in the next chapter) for your site, you might end up with a blank page if **templates** are not supported by your "theme".

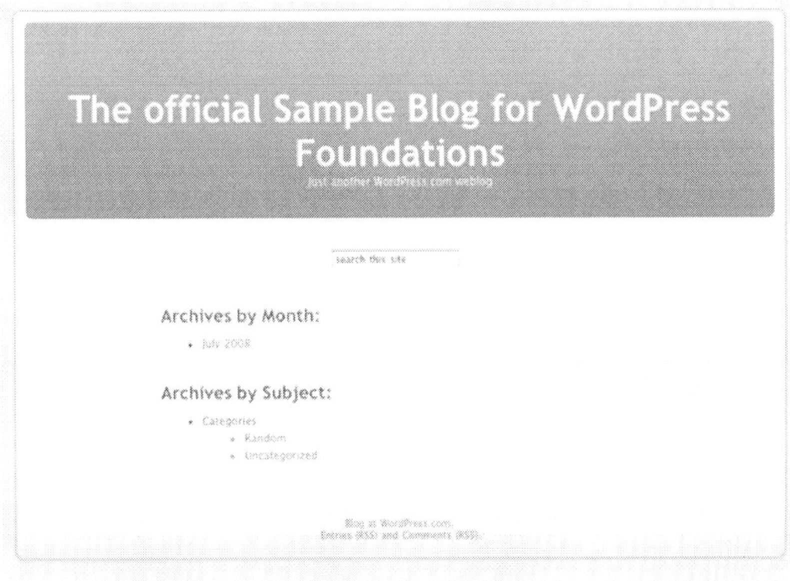

Chapter 8 Summary

In this chapter we learned what a Page is (a static page that is updated infrequently), some examples of how to use one:

Restaurant, update specials or menu, allow no comments.

Software Developer page for software, allows comments and trackbacks and updates to the latest version of the software.

We learned how to create a Page, we discussed templates, and that certain themes have additional templates, whilst some have none.

We learned a little about the Google Slap, and how to avoid it.

Chapter 8 Action Steps

- Create an About Us Page for your site
- Decide if you want to create any other pages for your site (and take the time to write them now, or at least come up with the names).
- If you will be using Googles PPC platform (Ad Words), or you plan on collecting any information (emails, or accepting payments), you need to create a Terms and Conditions, About Us, Contact Us, and a Privacy Policy so you can avoid getting “slapped”.
- If your blog is a personal blog, Terms and Privacy Policy are not needed, but a Contact Us and About us page allows your readers to get in touch with you, and learn more about you.

Chapter 9

Applying a theme

How To Choose And Apply a Theme For Your WordPress.com Blog

The default theme of WordPress, is something a lot of people are using. As such you may wish to differentiate yourself from the crowd by using a different theme. In this chapter I will show you 5 very flexible wordpress.com themes. At the end of the chapter, I will share with you a few more themes that are great for business.

If you're using WordPress.org and self-hosting your blog, then you will not have all of these themes available to you from the dashboard. You will have to install the themes individually. I go over how to do this in chapter 22. This chapter still applies to you, as the workflow is still the same.

Go to your dashboard, and click open the "Appearance" tab and choose "Themes" and you'll see your available themes.

Themes Widgets Extras Custom Image Header Color Header Edit CSS

Current Theme

Kubrick by Michael Heilemann

The default WordPress theme complete with customizable header and widgets.

OPTIONS: Widgets | Extras | Custom Image Header | Color Header | Edit CSS

Tags: two columns, fixed width, custom header, blue

Kubrick is the default theme for WordPress. If you scroll down below you will see (as of this writing) 5 pages full of themes. Go ahead and click on the name of the one displayed below. "Ambiru."

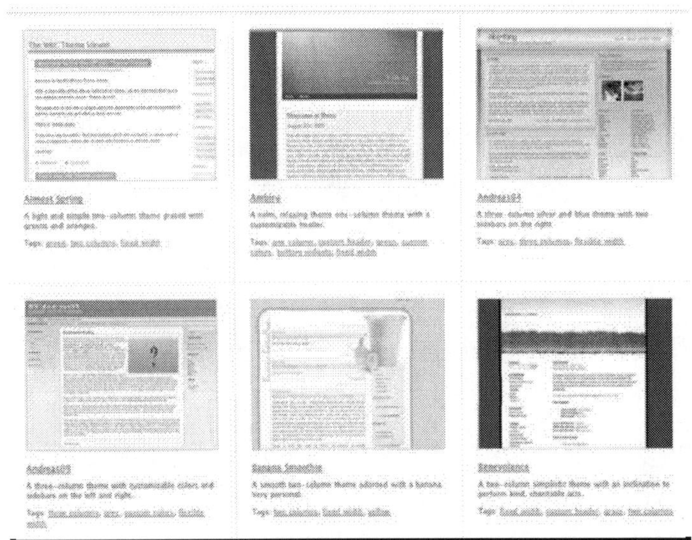

Ambiru

A calm, relaxing theme one-column theme with a customizable header.

Tags: one column, custom header, green, custom colors, bottom widgets, fixed width

When you click on it, you will see a preview of how your blog will look if you apply this theme. Go ahead and click the "activate" option on the top right, you can always go back to Kubrick or any other theme whenever you want.

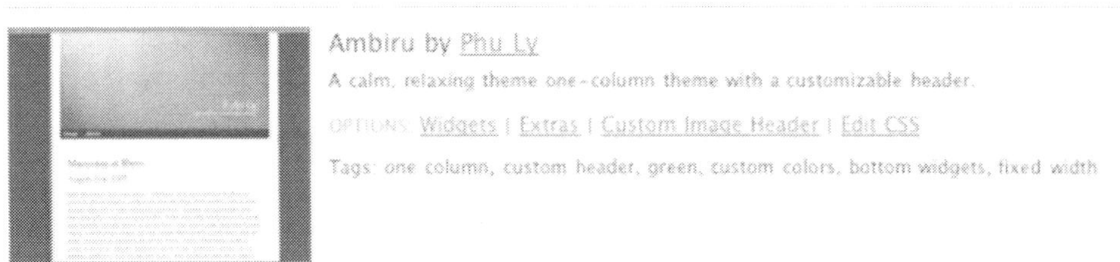

This is now your new theme. Go ahead and click "visit this site" to take a quick peek (I'll wait).

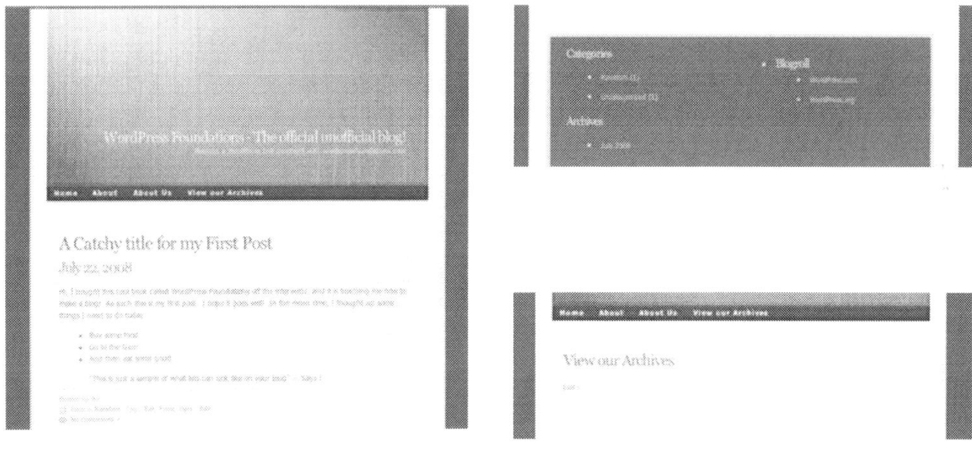

As you can see, your title is posted up top in the header, and your tag line is right below it.

The links to your pages are in the dark gray area (opposed to a sidebar). And you will also notice, your sidebar, and search function are no longer here.

If you look at the bottom you will see where your blog roll, and links to your archives are now placed.

Remember in the last chapter when we talked about pages, and how you need to be careful when you choose a "Page Template" as not all themes support it?

Go ahead and click View our Archives at the top.

As you can see, it is now "mysteriously" empty. Don't worry, when you switch back to Kubrick or any other theme that supports this "template" it will come back. That is why you need to be real careful when you change "themes" and take note if it breaks something. Then you will have to decide what is more important to you, that page, or the theme.

Lets go back and lets choose another really good theme.

Likely my favorite wordpress.com theme is, ChaoticSoul by Bryan Veloso. Click it and hit activate.

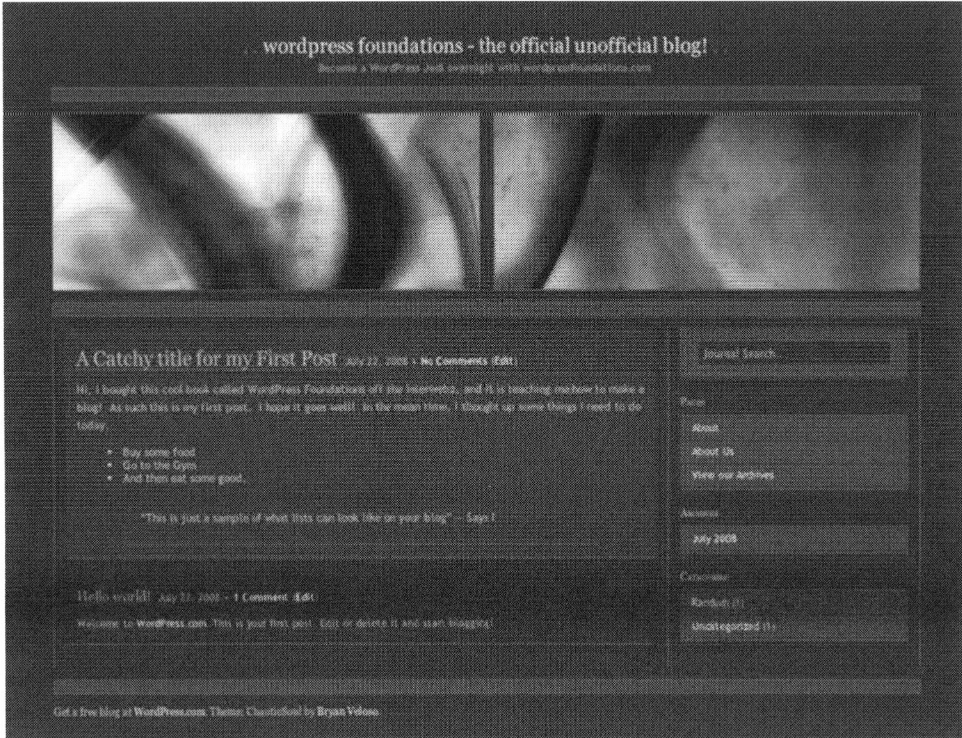

You will notice, we have search functionality again, the design looks cleaner, and we have access to our pages, archives, and categories on the far right.

If you click the "View Our Archives" function, you will notice that this theme does indeed support that "template".

Go back to your dashboard, and lets select another theme.

Another classic theme that I recommend is Hemingway by Kyle Neath.

Current Theme

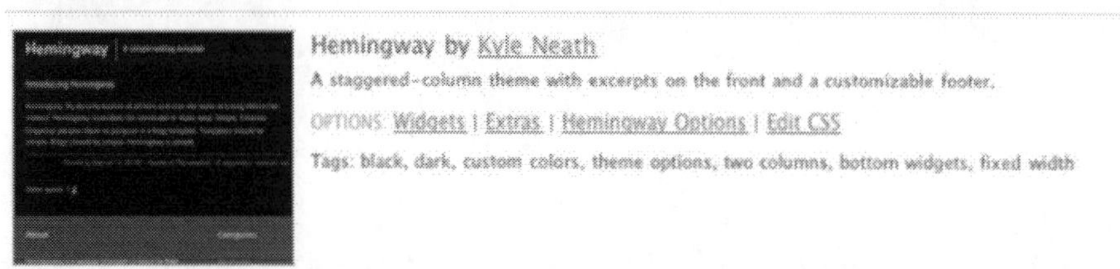

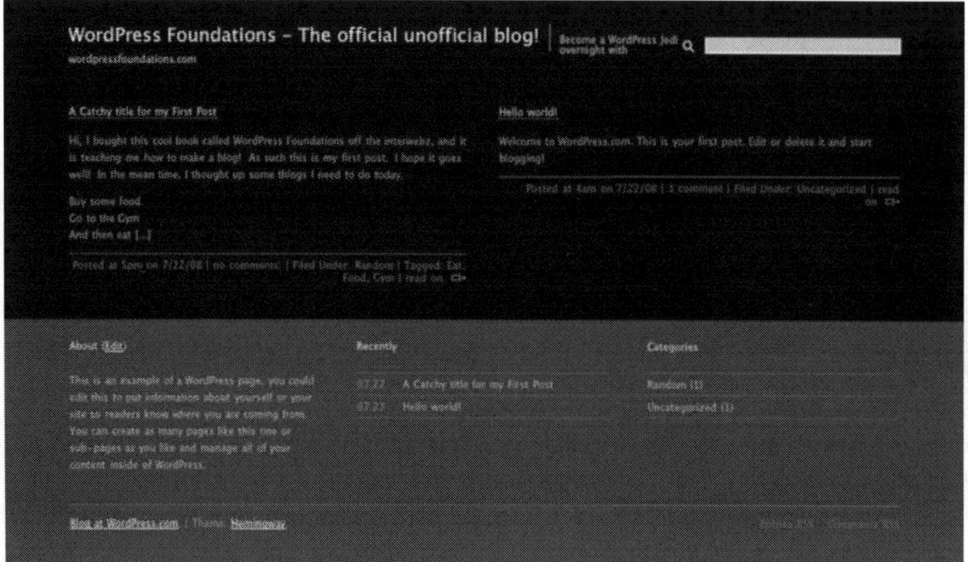

The down side about using this theme on wordpress.com is you don't have access to your pages by default. So it may or may not be for you

Go back to your dashboard, and lets choose another theme.

Select the theme called “Unsleepable” by Ben Gray. If you’re using the self-hosted version of WordPress, I highly recommend a customizable version of this called unwakeable. Lets activate the theme, and see how it looks.

Current Theme

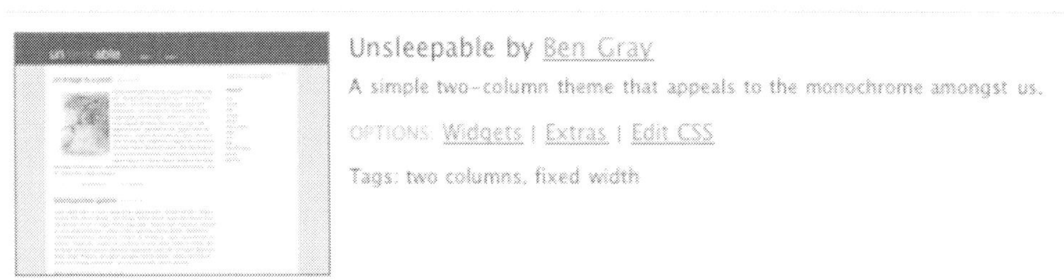

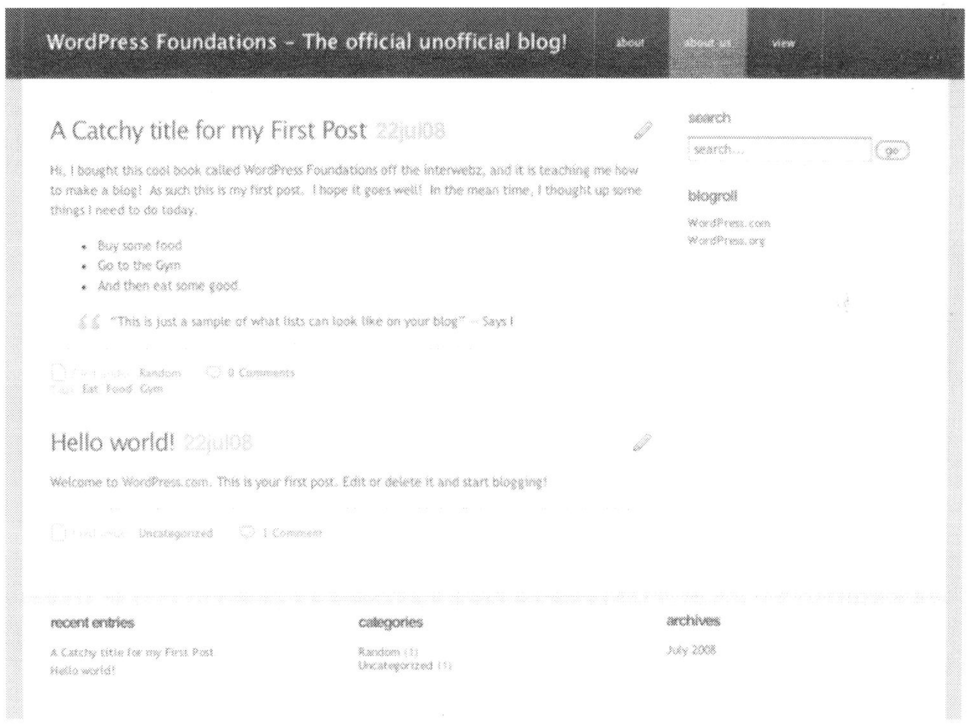

We have our "pages" at the top, and when you roll over the page, you will see it highlight (which is what I did to get this screen capture). You have your search, and on the bottom you have access to your archives, categories, and a quick list of recent entries.

This theme does not support our Archives Template. (Please note, this does not matter for us here, as there is no real reason to use an archive template page, when you have access to archives on your sidebar through a widget, which you can always add to your themes).

Go back to your dashboard, and lets pick one more theme.

Prologue.

This is a fun theme, I recommend it for people who are working on a project together, you can login, post and update and get back to work. I will show how this works, and create a custom entry via the front page of the blog!

The theme is called Prologue, it is by Joseph Scott, Matt Thomas, and Automattic (the makers of WordPress).

Current Theme

Prologue by Joseph Scott and Matt Thomas, Automattic

A group blog theme for short update messages, inspired by Twitter.

OPTIONS: Widgets | Extras | Custom Image Header | Edit CSS

Tags: blue, two columns, fixed width, custom header, microblog

WordPress Foundations - The official unofficial blog!

Hi, Anakin. Whatcha up to?

Tag it

Post it

Latest Updates RSS

Ani 5:44 pm on July 22, 2008 | 0 | # | e
Tags: Eat, Food, Gym

Hi, I bought this cool book called WordPress Foundations off the interwebz, and it is teaching me how to make a blog! As such this is my first post. I hope it goes well! In the mean time, I thought up some things I need to do today.

- Buy some food
- Go to the Gym
- And then eat some good.

"This is just a sample of what lists can look like on your blog" — Says I

Ani 4:41 am on July 22, 2008 | 1 | # | e

Welcome to **WordPress.com**. This is your first post. Edit or delete it and start blogging!

Recent Projects

Gym (1) RSS
Food (1) RSS
Eat (1) RSS

All Updates RSS

Blog at WordPress.com
Prologue theme by Automattic

On the top of the screen you see your avatar, and you have the option to post an update to your blog about what you're doing, as well as providing some tags.

This theme doesn't make use of categories by default, so instead post a tag. For example if your working on a game you could write, engine coding, or skinning the characters, etc. This way you can click those tags and see the updates based on those tags from various users. If you had more than one user, they would show up as well and display their avatar.

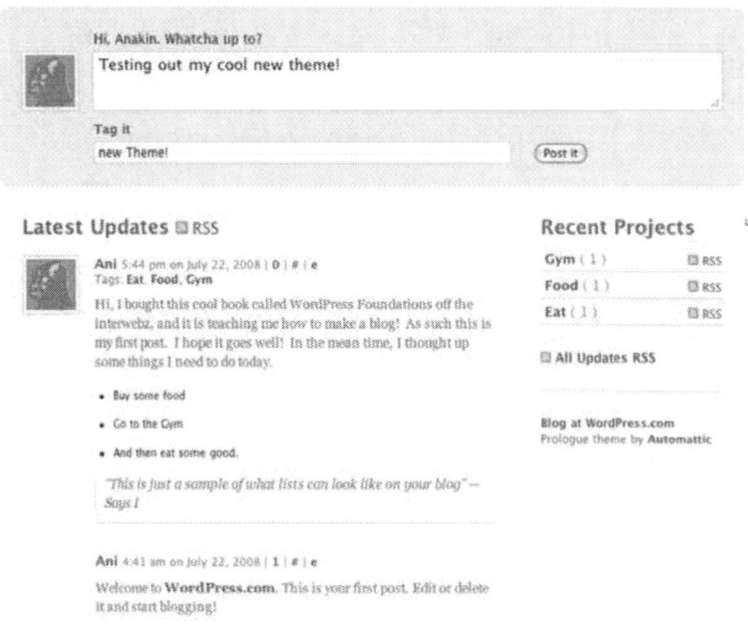

Here I'm filling out some information, as you can tell, I made a bad tag, I did this on purpose so we can delete the tag, and the post later on.

On the next page you can see what it looks like after you update the blog with your entry, you never leave the page, everything is done in real time, and quite smooth. Think of this theme as a microblogging theme. You can post quick updates easily, or you can post larger posts. This would be great to use as an internal blog to keep track with your projects.

Please note, when someone visits this site, they will not have the ability to post on your blog, it will not be an option, so no need to worry about people posting random stuff on your site, it is for users with logins only (to update their status).

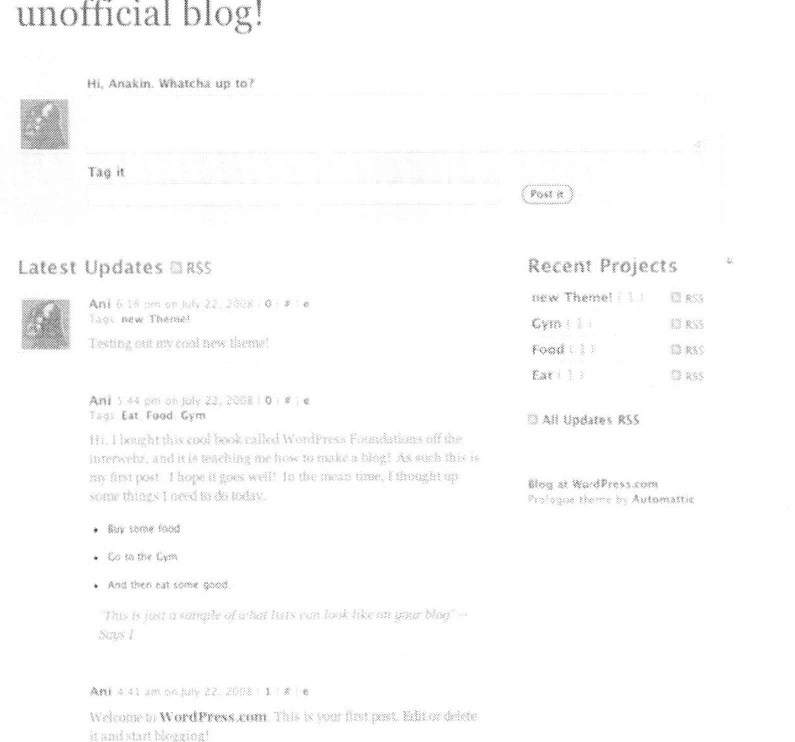

We have gone over 5 different themes, discussed the pros and cons of each, its time to pick one to continue on with this course. Please note, these were just five that I recommend, and enjoy using.

If you decide to use the self-hosted version of WordPress on your sever, you'll have access to THOUSANDS of themes.

Just remember, this is YOUR blog, do what you like, and express yourself. That's the only way to have fun.

I will continue using ChaoticSoul for this site.

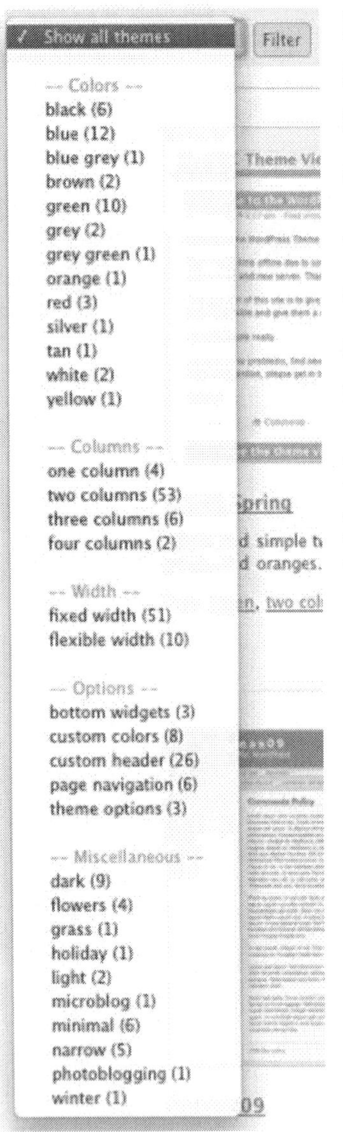

If you want a certain type of functionality for your theme please take advantage of the drop down menu functionality that allows you to sort by a certain feature.

You can sort by color, how many columns, whether the columns are fixed (not resizable) or flexible (can resize based on the users browser).

In the next section I'm going to share with you a few more really good themes that work great for professional websites.

10 More Themes

Here are 10 more highly recommended themes.

Contempt

Cutline

Emire

Fauna

Grid Focus

Light

MistyLook

PressRow

Simpla

The Journalist v1.3

Where to download thousands of themes freely

If you're using WordPress.org, you can download all of these themes and more by visiting the official WordPress theme site at:

wordpress.org/extend/themes/

Chapter 9 Summary

In this chapter we went over how to install a theme. I showed you 5 different themes, and walked you through them step by step. At the end of the chapter I showcased 10 more themes that are very useful.

To recap on installing a theme, visit dashboard, under appearance click "Themes", then click on a theme and press "Activate".

If you're using WordPress.org, you need to download the themes you wish to use first, unzip them, then upload the folder to your wordpress website in the themes folder inside wp-content.

Chapter 9 Action Steps

- Try out the themes I suggested.
- Try out a few other themes and see which ones you like the most, and which ones are more aligned with how you would like your website to look (think back to the exercise in chapter 2).
- Make notes of what you like, or don't like. (Specifically take note of the "sidebars")
- Remember that if you use WordPress.org and self-host, you have access to thousands of other themes.
- Find a theme that you like and activate it; in the next chapter we will cover how to modify it slightly using widgets.

Chapter 10

Widgets

What Exactly Is a Widget?

Widgets allow you to quickly and easily customize your site.

In this chapter, we will be covering how to set them up and change them. In a nutshell, all you do is choose a widget from the menu, and drag and drop it into the position that you would like it to appear in on your blog or site, click save, and your finished.

Adding Widgets To Your Site

Inside the dashboard, on the left side menu under Appearance click Widgets. Every time you select a theme, be aware that each theme already has its on set of widgets pre set. Whenever you go into the widgets menu, and add something, everything else gets erased on that theme (as far as widgets go, on your sidebars). It's a good idea to have your site open in a new window or tab prior to changing anything, so you can see where stuff was prior to modifying it.

Widgets provide you with a way to quickly and easily change your site. They are very easy to setup and the results are immediate.

You can revert back at anytime to "factory condition" specs by deleting the widgets you add to your site. When you do this, the default options will be restored.

Chapter 10 - Widgets

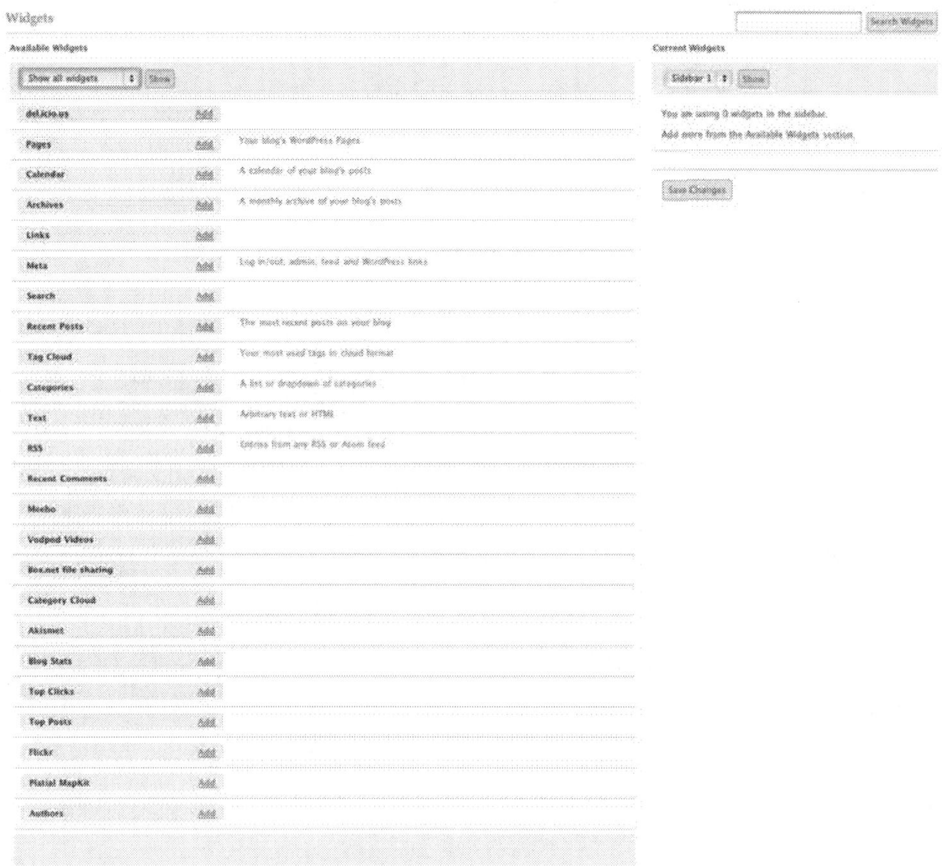

On the right you will see your sidebar, you can use the drop down menu and select which sidebar you want to work with.

This particular theme has 1 sidebar others have 2 or more.

By Default, this theme has: Search, Pages, Archives, and Categories.

To add a widget, just click "add" and it will appear to the right.

After you add a widget, you'll see it on the right. By clicking on the name and dragging, you can move the widget into whatever position you want.

Click "save changes" and then click view site to see the result.

Here is the search feature.

This is the calendar; the bright white text tells that we have posted something that day. When someone visits the site, they can scroll through the months, and click the date to see what you posted on that day.

These are our pages.

Lastly here are our links, which can be changed by editing the blog roll (checkout chapter 20 for more on editing Blog Rolls).

Here is our textbox, which is missing because we haven't typed anything in.

We now need to edit these widgets so they can provide more useful information.

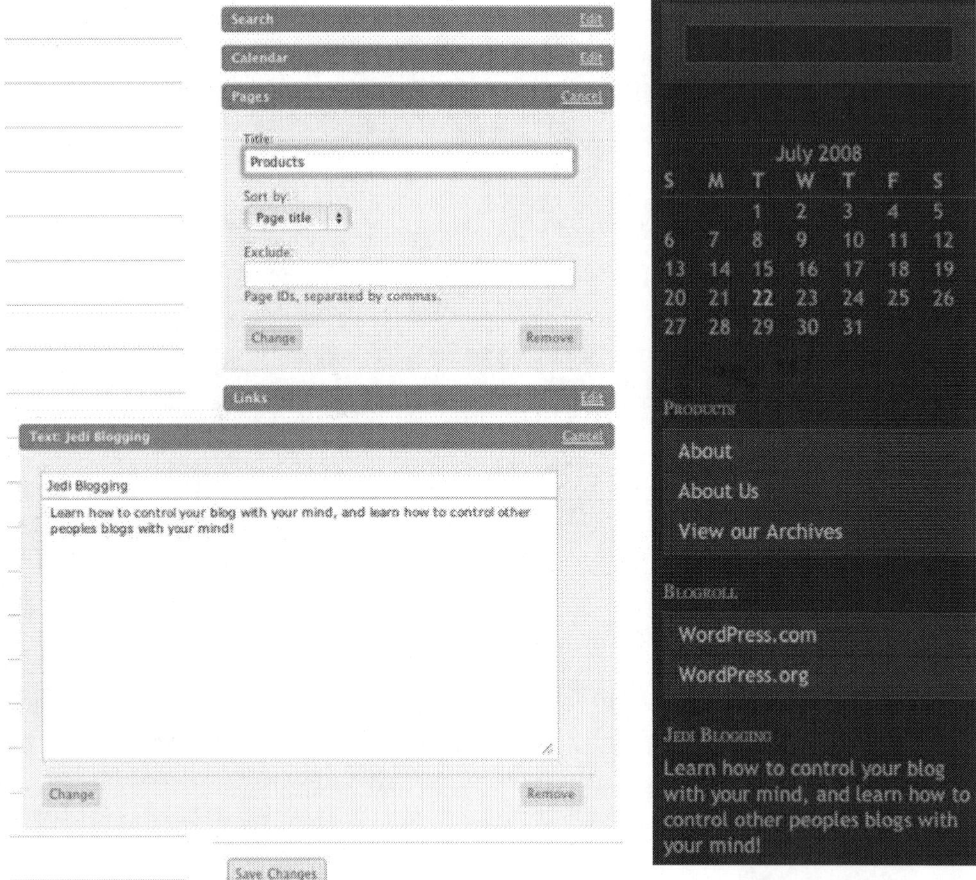

With this theme, we cannot have prewritten text in the search, change the blog roll name, or the calendar.

We can add text, and give our "pages" a name.

You can also use the text widget to input code (useful for ads).

Adding Custom Widgets

There are a lot of uses for adding widgets to your blog. In this chapter we have so far covered using the standard widgets that wordpress.com gives us.

If you want to showcase advertising on your blog, you can do so by creating a text widget and inserting HTML code.

If you're using WordPress.org, and you have a certain plugin enabled (like an ad rotator) you can insert that plugin specific code into a widget, and that widget will now show your plugin (opposed to having to modify the php files).

Another thing you can do is embed flash by using the widget (this can be a flash movie, a game, an advertisement, or a flash widget that displays your nike+ stats, your weight loss stats, your twitter updates, etc, etc.

The possibilities are endless. By using widgets, you now have the power to modify your blog to your hearts content without having to worry about learning how to code.

In seconds you can completely change your site and add all new levels of interactivity to your blog.

Chapter 10 Summary

In chapter 10 we learned about Widgets. You now know what they are, and how you can really take advantage of them to take command of your blog.

To recap, a widget allows you to quickly and easily add additional features to your blog with little to no technical skills required.

You visit dashboard and under appearance you select Widgets.

From here you can add any widget you want, or create a text widget and add HTML code which will let you embed ads, display flickr photos, showcase twitter updates, link to your myspace, facebook or linked in, etc, etc.

Chapter 10 Action Steps

- Organize your site to look the way you want.
- In chapter 2 you visited several sites and took note of what you liked most, in the last chapter you noticed what you liked most about each theme (and paid attention to the sidebars), now that you know about the power of widgets, I want you to modify and setup your site the way you want before proceeding to the next chapters.
- Add any widgets that you feel add to your site. Remember, widgets can be deleted as easily as added, so have fun!

Chapter 11

WordPress.com Extras & Upgrades

What is an extra?

This is a feature added for wordpress.com (only). Right now, it only provides two options, which we will now cover. If you're using **WordPress.org**, you can skip this chapter and **skip to chapter 14**.

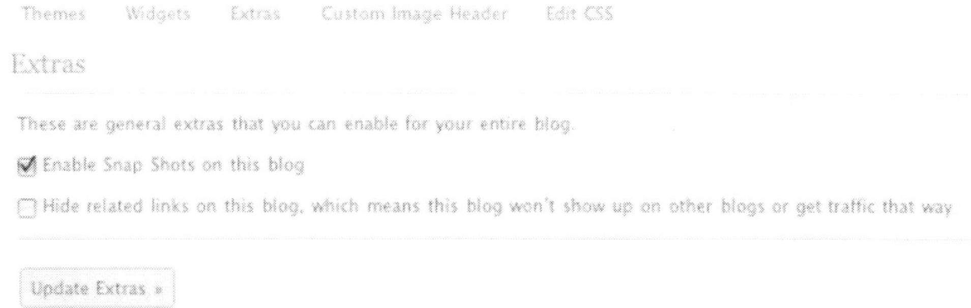

The first option is to Enable Snap Shots on your blog. What is this? Whenever you hover over a link, it will automatically preview that link, so you can see what it looks like prior to clicking it.

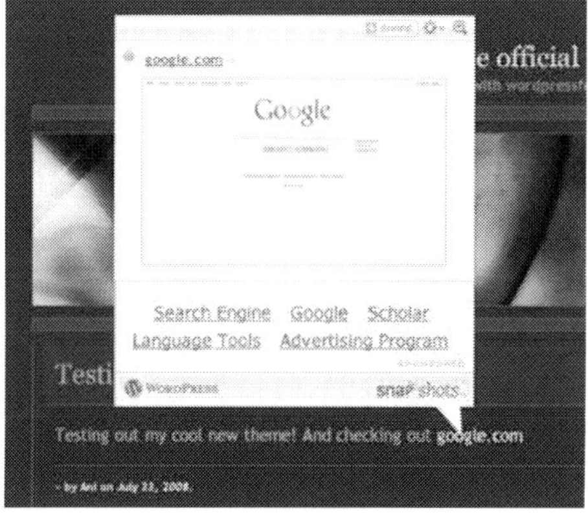

The second option is hiding related links on this blog.

This feature is turned on by default (thus showing other related links on your blog). When you look at the bottom of a post, you will see "possible related posts" that are on other blogs on the wordpress.com domain.

If you leave this on, when someone visits your site, and enjoys an article, at the bottom they will get directed to another blog with similar content on the network, and as such away from you!

If you leave this on, then you get advertised on other blogs that have this feature turned on, so the choice is up to you. If you want to reach more people, you may want to leave this on, as it can only help.

WordPress.com Upgrades

Upgrades, are additional features you can purchase for your wordpress.com blog. To view these features, go to your dashboard and choose upgrades (it's at the bottom on the menu on the left).

Before you spend money on WordPress.com upgrades, I encourage you to consider self-hosting your blog and using WordPress.org. All the features you're paying for here are available (and much more) on the wordpress.org platform.

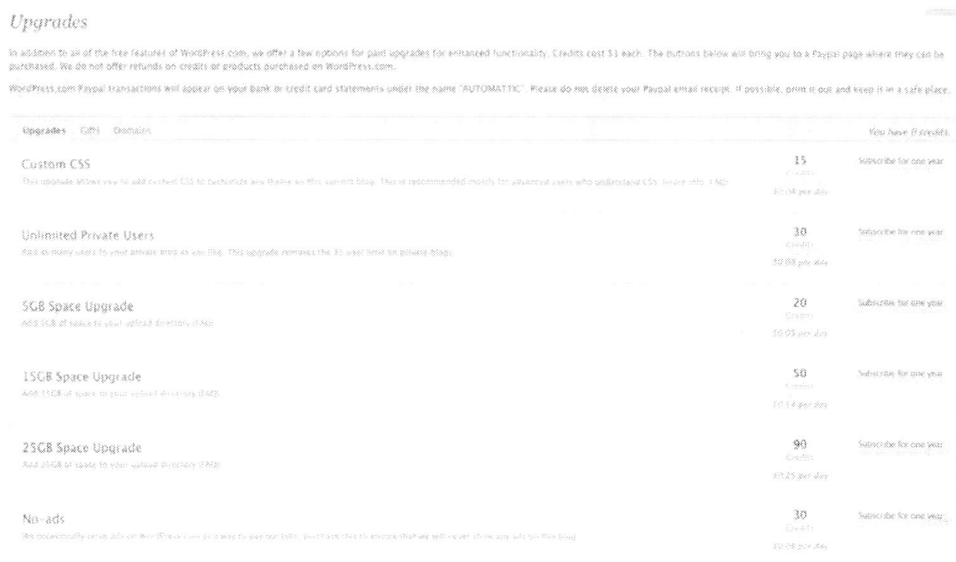

A "Credit" is the form of currency for wordpress.com. Each Credit is equal to one dollar USD.

Custom CSS, lets you change the CSS of your blog, giving you much more creative control over how your blog looks.

Unlimited Private User's means you can add more than 35 people to your blog.

The rest of your options are space upgrades, if your uploading a lot of files, such as photos and PDFs, you may need to upgrade your account to get more space (you have three gigs by default).

Gifts are for buying these items for other users on wordpress.com

The Domains option allows to you have your wordpress.com blog point to your domain. You are given the nameserver information to input on your domain name, so when a user types in yourblog.com, he does not see yourblog.wordpress.com.

This feature is 10 dollars a year, and is worth doing if you do not wish to pay for a hosting account, and want to keep your blog on WordPress.com.

You are not charged until the forwarding is working (at least at the time of this writing).

Chapter 11 Summary

In this chapter you learned what WordPress.com Extras and Upgrades are. This is a WordPress.com feature only.

Chapter 11 Action Steps

- Decide if you need any of these extras or upgrades
- Remember that you can use wordpress.org and self host to get all of these features, and a whole lot more (but there is some overhead).
- If you love WordPress and want to support them, the best way to do so (for you and them) is to visit them at wordpress.org/donate and send them a donation (I think if you enjoy using WordPress, regardless the platform, you should consider donating to help them out). It is not required.

Chapter 12

Custom Image Header

Introduction to the Custom Image Header

Through the use of the "Custom Image Header" you can import your own graphics into the website and have them displayed at the top. (This is under Appearance.) This is WordPress.com ONLY.

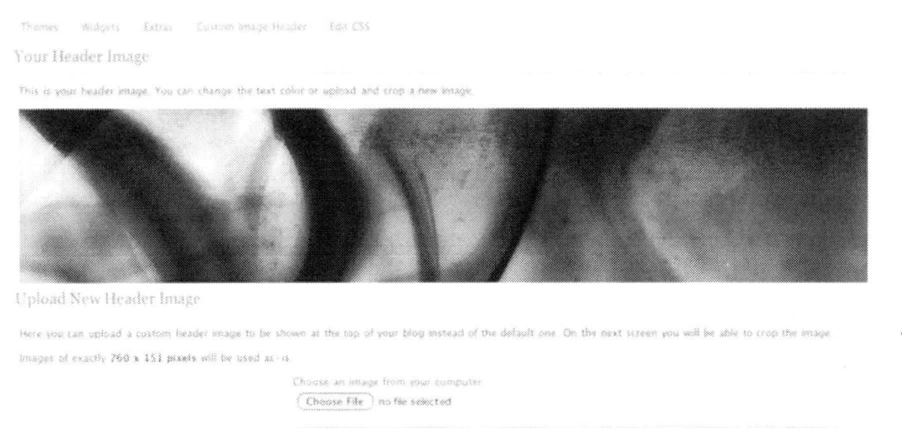

This theme requires your image dimensions to be 760x151. Each theme varies, and some do not support this feature at all.

This particular theme, will split the image in half, and show it on the two bars, so we need to make an image composition inside of Photoshop, gimp, or any of your favorite image editors.

If you were to upload an image larger than these dimensions you would be get the same menu you got before when you uploaded your avatar image. Lets start by adding a really large image, and cropping it in WordPress.

Click "choose an image from your computer" --> then select the jpg you want to add, and then click *Upload*.

I will use the same image I used before, to keep things simple.

Again, you want to choose part of your image, based on the "marching ants" or dotted lines in the rectangle.

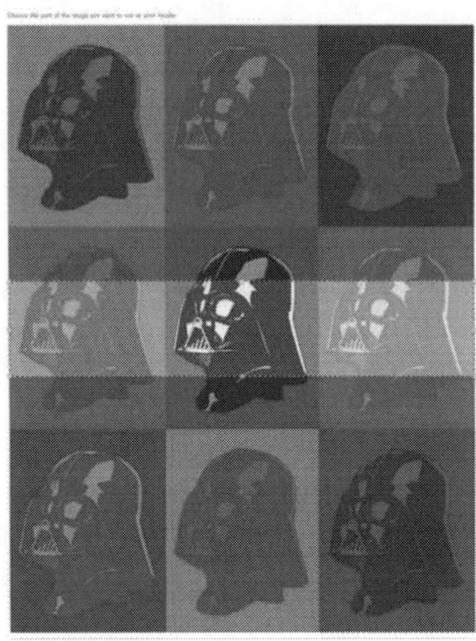

Only resize from the corners (top left, top right, bottom left, bottom right,) as these will allow you to keep your dimensions and not skew your image.

When you are done, on the bottom click "Crop Header".

Themes Widgets Extras Custom Image Header Edit CSS

Header complete!

Visit your site and you should see the new header now.

You will be informed that the header has been cropped, and to visit your site to see how it looks.

When you visit your site you will see your header at the top.

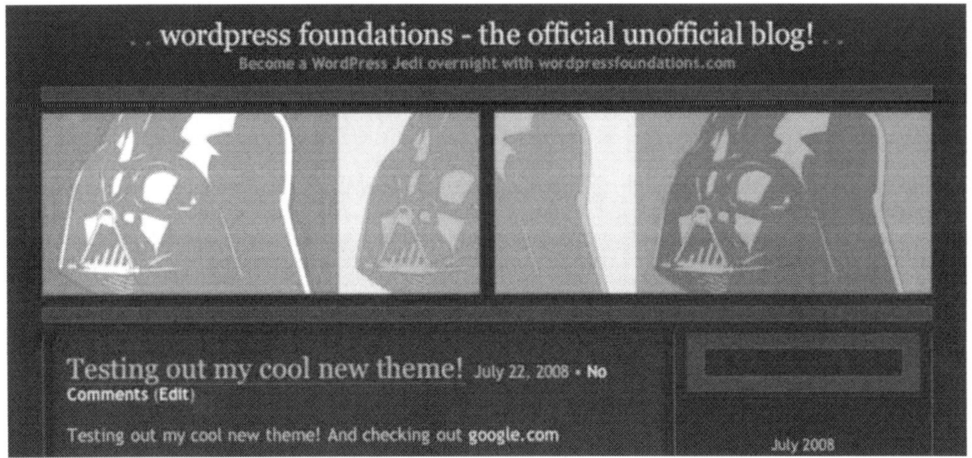

As you can tell, this doesn't quite work with this theme. I will edit this photo in another application, to make it fit better with this theme.

I wrote out very detailed instructions, step by step on how to edit this photo, using the Internet, with no external application, meaning you can edit the photo anywhere in the world, on any kind of computer, all you need is internet access.

As this is a book about WordPress and not image manipulation, I'm not including that part in this book. However you sign up for my newsletter at EnlightenedWebmastery.com and get it there.

It's 11 pages, and covers applying special effects (to tone down the image), and edit it so we can get the image to work with this theme (using 4 small images, opposed to 1 very large one).

I showcase each step, in detail, teaching you why and how I went about creating the image, why I used the tools I did, and how to use them.

You can skip doing this if you want, it's not necessary, I just thought it would be useful to show how to do this for free, anywhere in the world, no experience necessary.

I should also note, it would be much simpler to do the whole effect in Photoshop or the gimp, but not everyone has those programs, or the desire to learn them.

Hence the completely free method I laid out in the book. Please check it out, and feel free to tell me what you think.

Chapter 12 Summary

This chapter introduced you to the Custom Image Header function (which is WordPress.com specific). You learned how to upload an image and how to crop it to fit. In the next chapter we will upload our fixed image (after following along with the special report).

Chapter 12 Action Steps

- Create a logo for your website.
- A simple logo creation tip is, make your image contrasty, think thick and thin, wide or small, big and little, black and red.
- You can checkout my special report for more information.

Chapter 13

Custom Image Header Part 2

Putting up your custom header

In the special report you can get from my website, we went over a workflow for taking an image and manipulating it to better fit our design goals, and now we are ready to put this on our blog, as the official header.

Go to your dashboard, and click on Appearance -> custom image header.

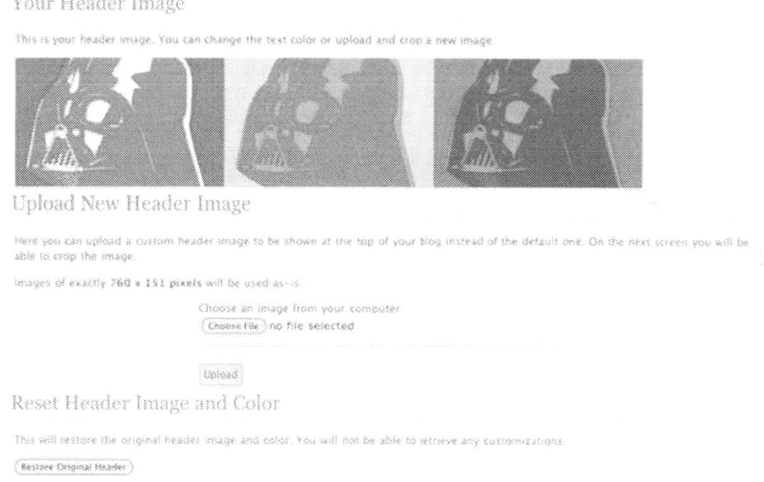

This is what our current image looks like. What you need to do is click "choose file" and load up the new header you just saved in the special report. Then click upload. (To revert back to the original graphic, click "restore original header").

Now you need to crop the photo, just as we did last time.

Choose the part of the image you want to use as your header.
Crop Header

When you're finished, you'll get a box saying "Header Complete", now go visit the site to see how it looks.

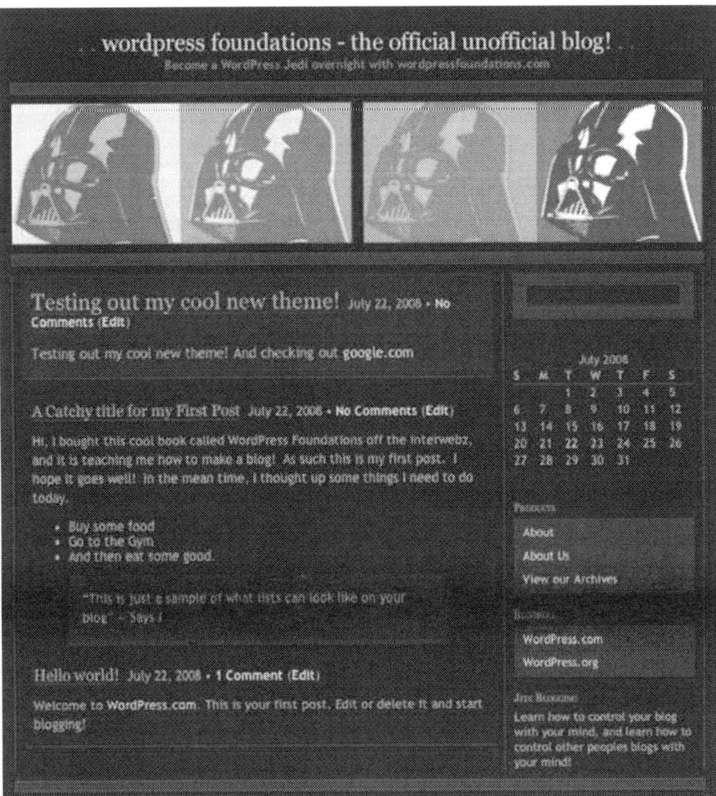

Here is what the site looks like now.

Since I'm not going to keep this image on my blog, I will be restoring the original image header.

To restore your custom image header back to its original form click "restore original header".

Chapter 13 Summary

This chapter picks up after chapter 12 and the special report.

In chapter 12 you learned what the Custom Image Header was, and what to keep in mind. In the special report, we created a custom image to use for our blog. In this chapter we uploaded the new image to our blog.

At the end of the chapter we learned how to revert back to the original image.

Chapter 13 Action Steps

- Take the graphic that you created after following the special report and reading chapter 12 and upload it to your site.
- Your site is now branded.

Chapter 14

Comments

Introduction to chapter 14

This chapter deals with comments. You will learn how to enable comments, how to moderate them, and how to handle comments in general.

Comments are a very important aspect of your website that should not be overlooked. By allowing your readers to participate in conversations with you or other readers, it creates a community that gives them reason to come back and visit your site.

This chapter also teaches you how to deal with spam so you can make sure your site is not filled with spammy comments.

Why Should I Enable Comments?

The main point of a blog in today's world is to communicate. When you post an article, and others read it, they like to share their insights with you, as well as other people. When they leave a post, it gives them incentive to check back to see what others wrote.

Someone could want to ask you a question about your post, or thank you, for helping him or her out with a problem.

For this reason I always recommend allowing comments, and to have them automatically posted. I go through a couple times a day checking for spam, and deleting posts that do not add to the discussion, I recommend you do the same.

Here is an example of how comments look on your blog.

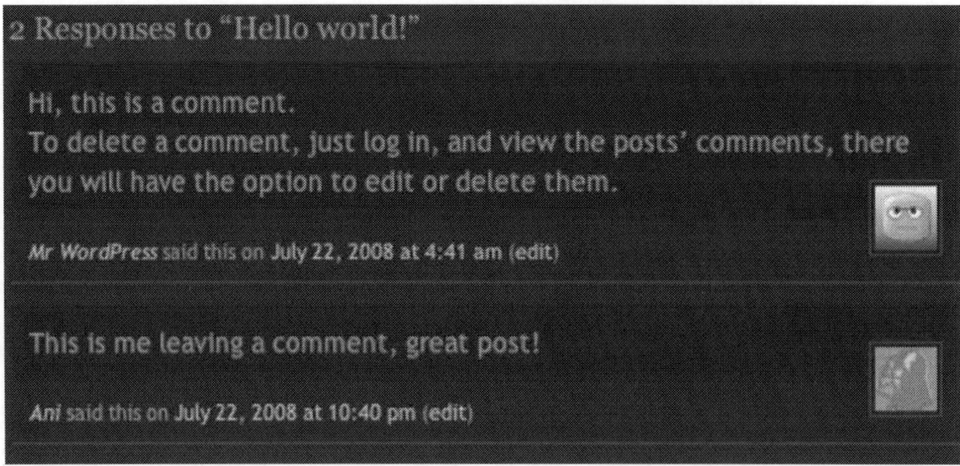

You need to be careful about your comments though, as I posted back in the chapter on writing posts, some people will try and spam your blog. One of the best things to do, is keep track of your comments, and delete anything that seems like spam.

If someone wrote that last post, I would definitely delete it! It adds nothing to the post. If he said Great Post, thanks, that would be different.

How to Enable Comments?

Visit your dashboard and on the left hand menu, under settings click discussion.

From here you can choose to enable comments, as well as waiting times. (Check Chapter 6 for more information.)

How to View Your Comments?

Go to your dashboard, and click comments. If you have the Recent Comments module running, you can also access your most recent ones from there.

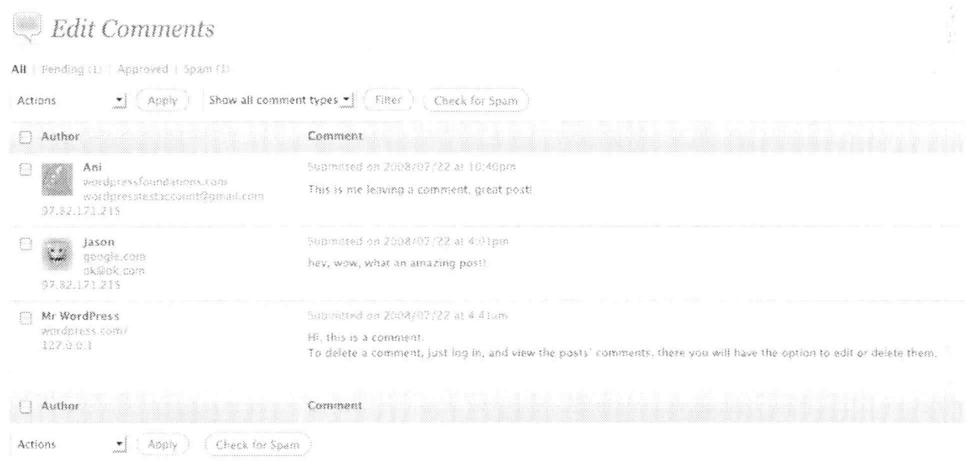

You can see the users name, his website, and his email, in case you need to contact him. You can also see his post.

Hover over each comment and you will be able to approve a comment, mark it as spam, or delete it.

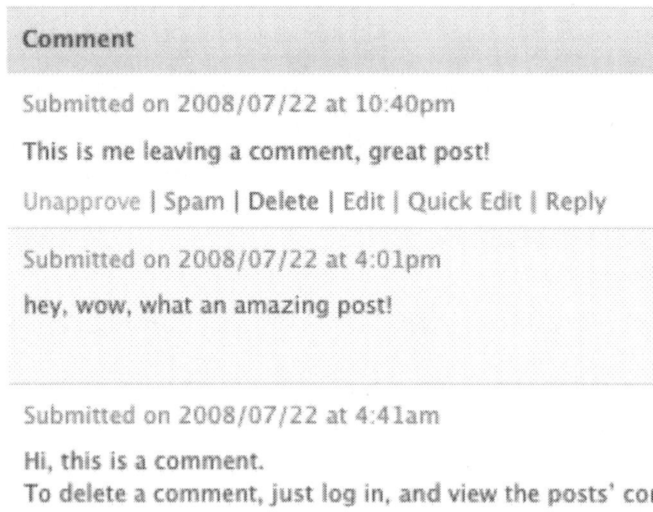

You can decide to unapprove a previously approved comment incase you wanted to edit the comment or contact the author prior to posting.

You can edit the post by clicking on edit.

If you click on the "Akismet Spam" box you can check comments that the filter has picked up, this can ensure that no real comment accidently got tagged as spam. Spam is deleted automatically in 15 days.

Chapter 14 Summary

In this chapter you learned why you might want to enable comments (to create a sort of community and give readers a reason to check back on that post), and so you can communicate with your readers and give them more information or help.

You learned about spam and some ways to handle it (this was covered in detail in chapter 6).

You learned how to enable comments (by clicking discussion under settings on your dashboard) and you learned how to use the new comments module on your dashboard.

Chapter 14 Action Steps

- Decide if you want to enable comments
- Make a plan for how often you will "clean up" your comments.
- Check back to chapter 6 for more information on what each of the menu items for discussion settings mean.

Chapter 14 - Comments

Chapter 15

Adding Multimedia to your blog

What All Types of Multimedia Can I Add To My Blog

In this chapter, you're going to learn how to add multimedia to your site. You'll learn how to add videos from youtube, how to add photos, as well as mp3s or pdfs. You'll learn how to add images to your site so you stay within the bounds of the law (and only use images that you're allowed to use on your site). At the end of the chapter, I'll share some additional resources.

How To Insert Images

Adding images to your articles, greatly improves the chances someone will read your post. It's less intimidating than a large block of text, and very easy to fix. I'll go over 2 different ways of how to add pictures, and share the pros and cons of each method.

First, we are going to add an image from amazon.com, and add it to our post.

Go to your dashboard, and write a new page, create a title, and insert some text.

I'm going to use text from a review I wrote for a product on amazon.com.

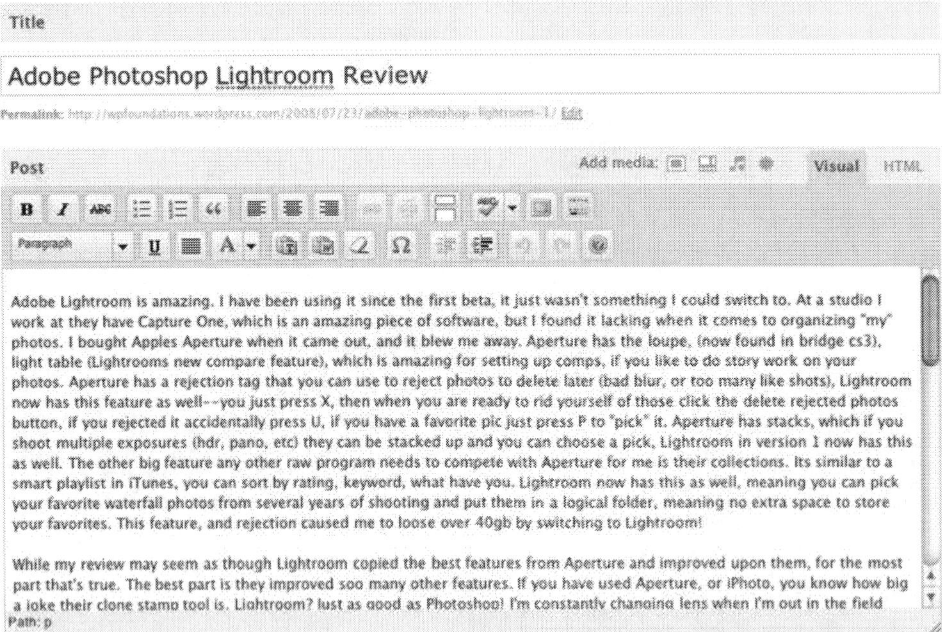

If I go ahead and preview this post (by clicking preview), you can see how uninteresting and intimidating it looks as pure text.

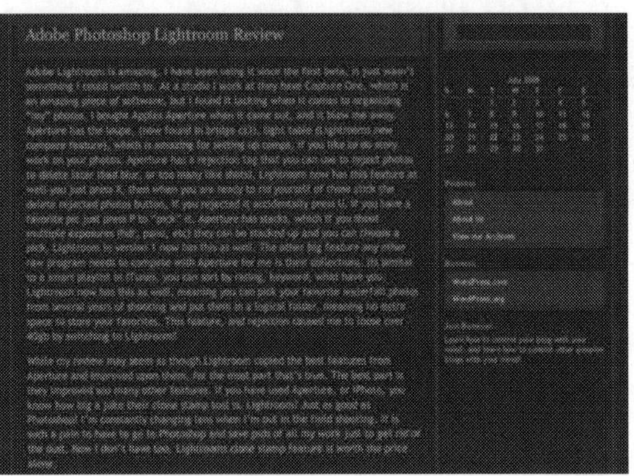

Now we'll insert an image. From within the visual editor, move your mouse to the location where you want to add an image and click on the insert / edit image option.

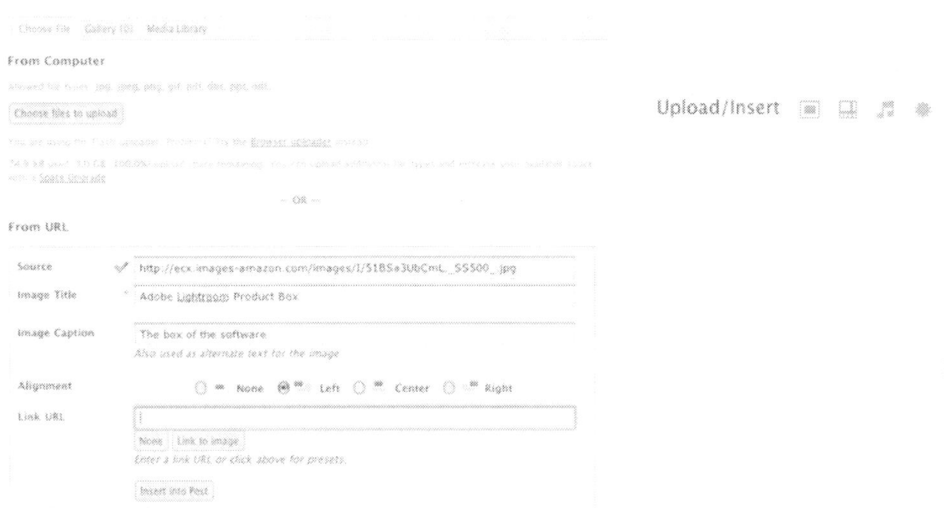

Put the URL in. Give it a descriptive name, give the image a caption, then choose how your alignment. Then click Insert into post. (To add your own image, choose the top option)

This is a very large image, and doesn't look the way I intended, so lets change it.

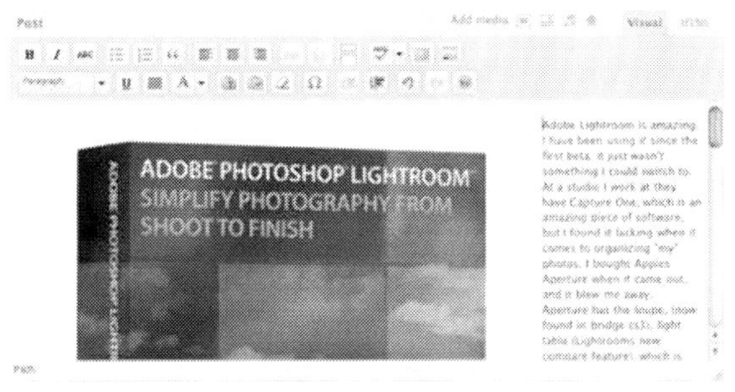

Highlight the image, and click the "Edit Image" button.

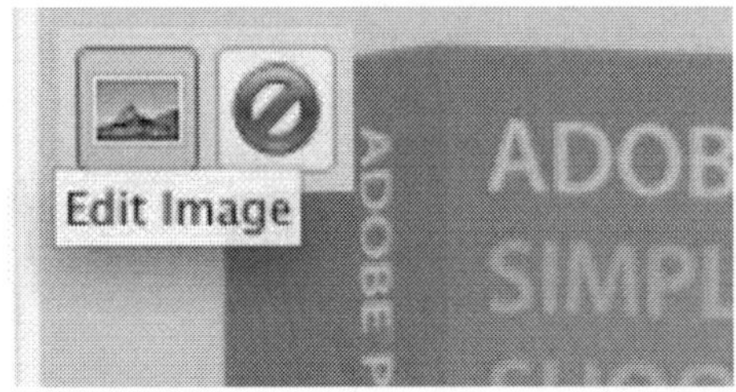

You can dynamically adjust the image based on percentage and let WordPress calculate the dimensions for you, while keeping track of how it looks in the preview above.

If you want to display the image at a certain size, click advanced, and type in a number, then click update.

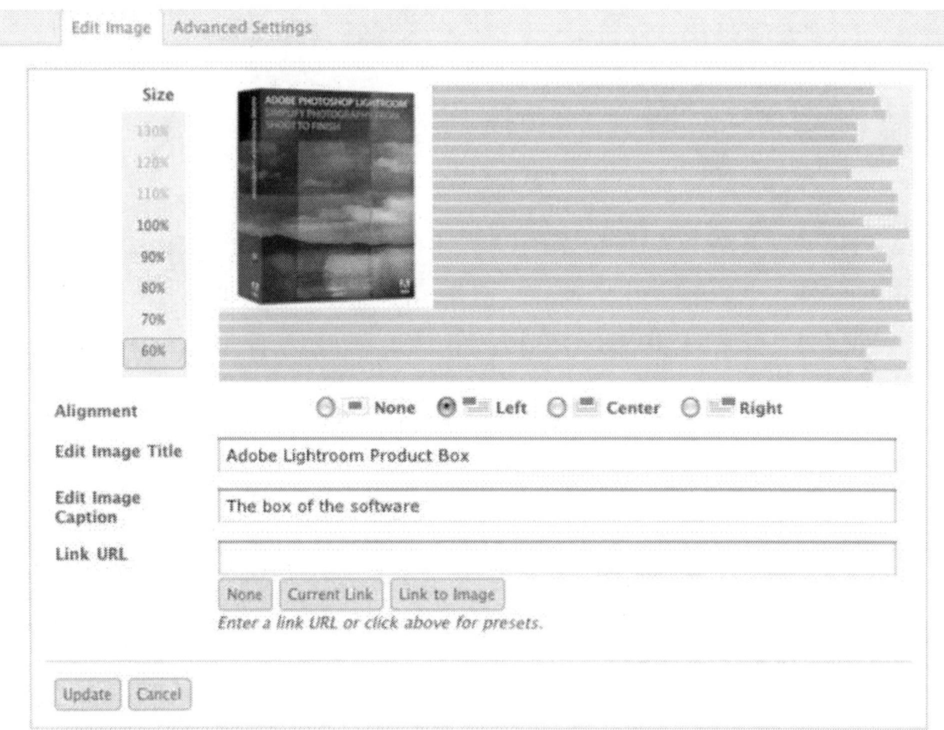

Here, I'll change it to 250x250, and click update.

Advanced Image Settings

Source *	http://ecx.images-amazon.com/images/I/51BSa3UbCmL._SS500_.jpg
Edit Alternate Text	The box of the software
Size	Width 250 Height 250 Original Size
CSS Class	alignleft
Styles	
Image properties	Border Vertical space Horizontal space

Adobe Lightroom is amazing. I have been using it since the first beta, it ju
wasn't something I could switch to. At a studio I work at they have Capture
One, which is an amazing piece of software, but I found it lacking when it
comes to organizing "my" photos. I bought Apples Aperture when it came
out, and it blew me away. Aperture has the loupe, (now found in bridge
cs3), light table (Lightrooms new compare feature), which is amazing for
setting up comps, if you like to do story work on your photos. Aperture ha:
a rejection tag that you can use to reject photos to delete later (bad blur, o
too many like shots), Lightroom now has this feature as well--you just pre
X, then when you are ready to rid yourself of those click the delete rejectec
photos button, if you rejected it accidentally press U, if you have a favorite
pic just press P to "pick" it. Aperture has stacks, which if you shoot multipl
exposures (hdr, pano, etc) they can be stacked up and you can choose a
pick, Lightroom in version 1 now has this as well. The other big feature an
other raw program needs to compete with Aperture for me is their
collections. Its similar to a smart playlist in iTunes, you can sort by rating,

This is much better, but still to large, I think one more time will do it!

In the next image you can see that I moved the slider down to 60% and it made it even smaller, in this case, 150x150. I think it looks better.

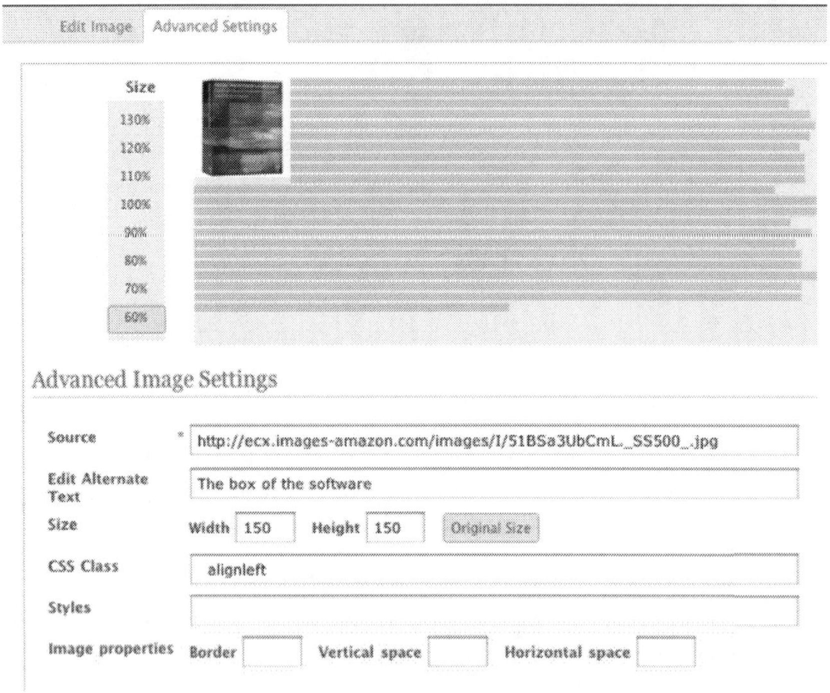

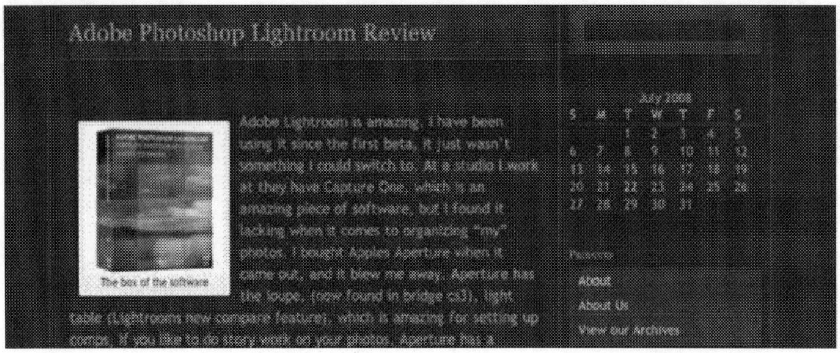

I think you will agree, this is much more agreeable.

Adding Images Throughout the Body of Your Article

Lets show another way to do this, and go over adding an image using an alternate alignment.

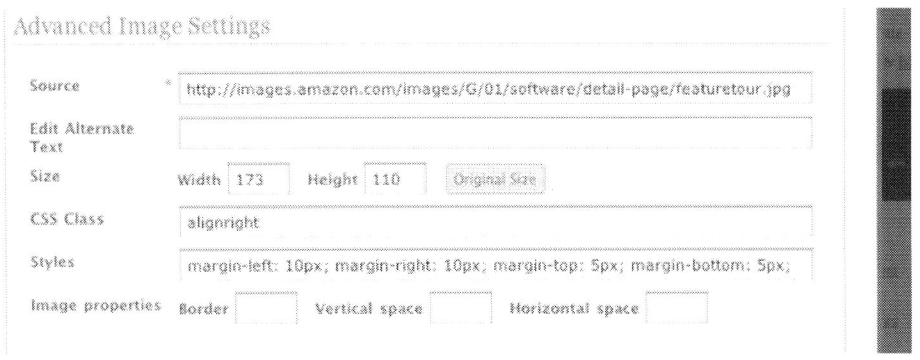

This image is right aligned, and I adjusted the alignment, adding some vertical and horizontal space to get it to look better in the post.

On this image, I left aligned it, lowered the size of the image, and set the vertical space to 5 and put the horizontal at 10. This gives the image some additional space around the text.

Here is what the final post looks like, adding 3 images. I think it reads better.

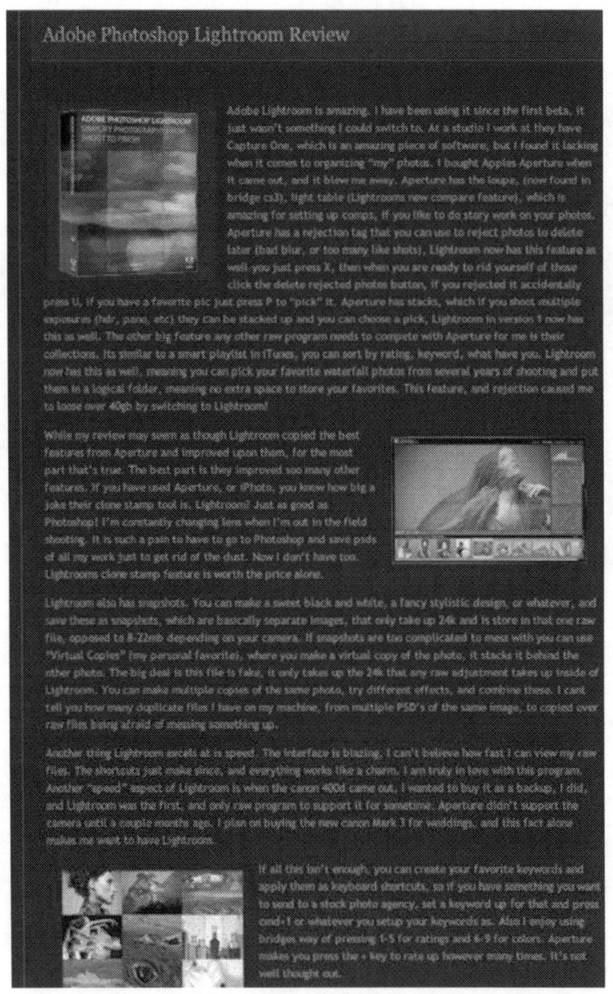

The second way of adding an image, is uploading an image from your computer, and inserting it onto your blog.

If you are going to be uploading photos that you just took with your digital camera, I encourage you to use some software to reduce the size of those images; 1200x1200 should be the largest any image should be for the web.

The images on this post are all under 200x200, try to keep the images from being to large. Set them so that when a user clicks on an image, it will load up the larger image. I suggest trying to keep the image size down to 700 pixels wide (or less). If you're making a photoblog, there is no need in having such a large size for an image, as it forces the visitor to wait longer to load up your page, and the longer they wait, the sooner they will just walk away.

You can download your photos from your digital camera and open in Photoshop, and adjust the image size (ctrl + alt + I or cmd + option + I), and save that (then upload to an image hosting account, and link to your image on your blog). (view chapter 2 for services)

I'm going to add my picture under the about me page, and show how to do it.

In your dashboard, click Pages -> Edit -> then click About Us.

In your post choose a location for the image and click insert image.

Click on the "choose files to upload", and select your image.

Fill in the information as necessary.

I'm leaving the link URL in there, with that being there, you can click on the image to view the image in full size.

Click insert into post, and it's now on your page.

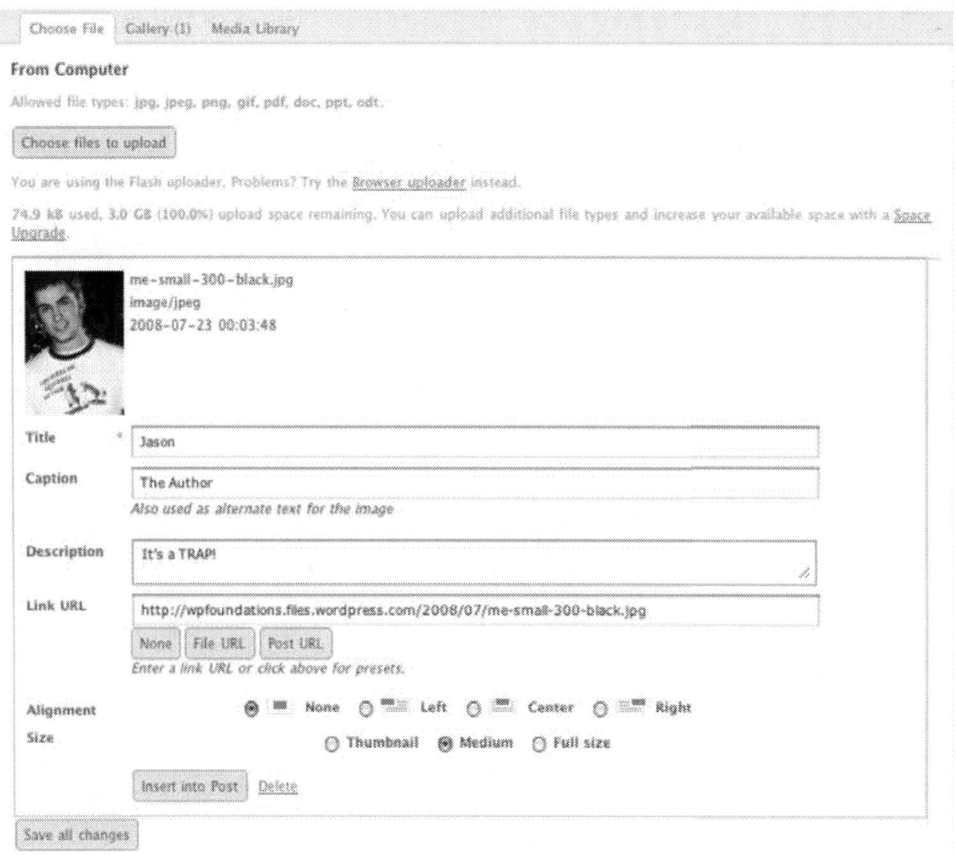

The image is quite large, so lets go back and adjust the size the way we did before.

I had to make this quite small to get it work right. Here are the settings, and the final output.

Edit Image | Advanced Settings

Size

130%
120%
110%
100%
90%
80%
70%
60%

Advanced Image Settings

Source: http://wpfoundations.wordpress.com/files/2008/07/me-small-300-black.jpg?w=214

Edit Alternate Text: The Author

Size: Width 50 Height 70 Original Size

CSS Class: size-medium wp-image-20 alignright

Styles

Image properties: Border Vertical space Horizontal space

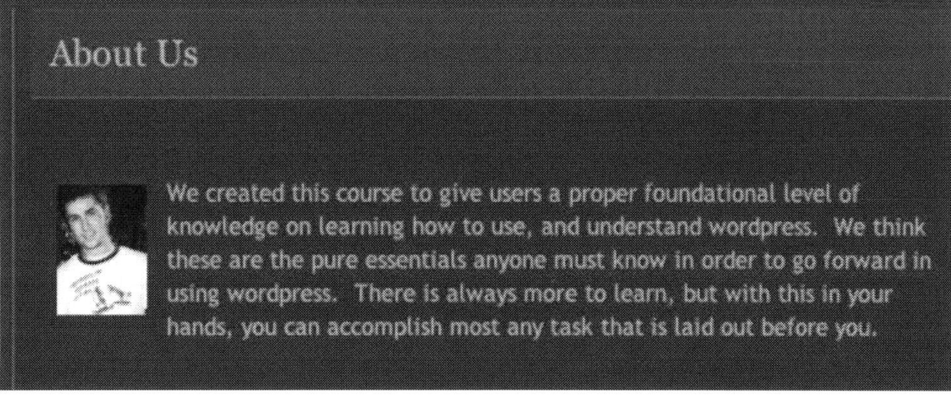

About Us
We created this course to give users a proper foundational level of knowledge on learning how to use, and understand wordpress. We think these are the pure essentials anyone must know in order to go forward in using wordpress. There is always more to learn, but with this in your hands, you can accomplish most any task that is laid out before you.

Warning about adding images to your website.

When you are adding images to your blog, you need to make sure that you own the copyright to that image, or that it is in the public domain, or is copyright free.

If you want to make sure you get images you can post on your website (news sites are generally a safe bet). You can buy photos from *http://www.istockphoto.com* or check out the following site for free images.

http://search.creativecommons.org/

Of further note, please understand, when you are linking your images from another website (opposed to hosting them on your own site) you're stealing that persons bandwidth, which is not nice, and if the website changes the name of the image, or deletes it, your site will have missing images, and can confuse people, as it is unlikely you will notice that this has happened 6 months from now.

Adding Video From Youtube.com

You can add video the same way you added the image previously, you do so by clicking the "add video" button.

Go to YouTube.com, and find a video that you enjoy, and copy the URL (you cannot use the embed code on wordpress.com, so use the URL). Please note if you are using wordpress.org, you can use the embed code. (Check the end of this chapter for a tutorial.)

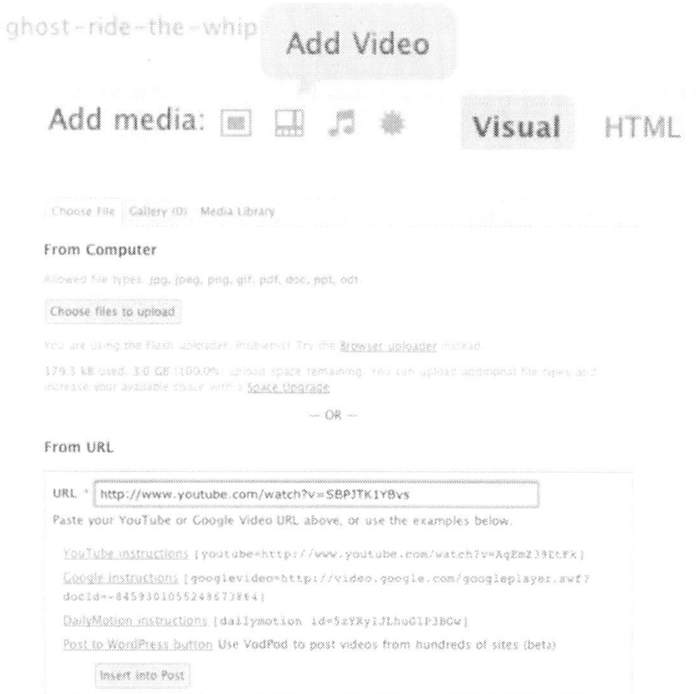

Click "Add Video" then Input the URL, and click insert into post.

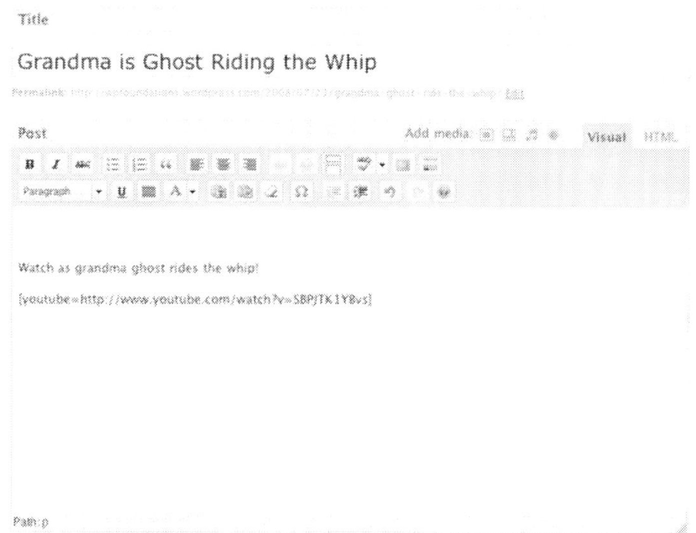

Insert some text then click publish.

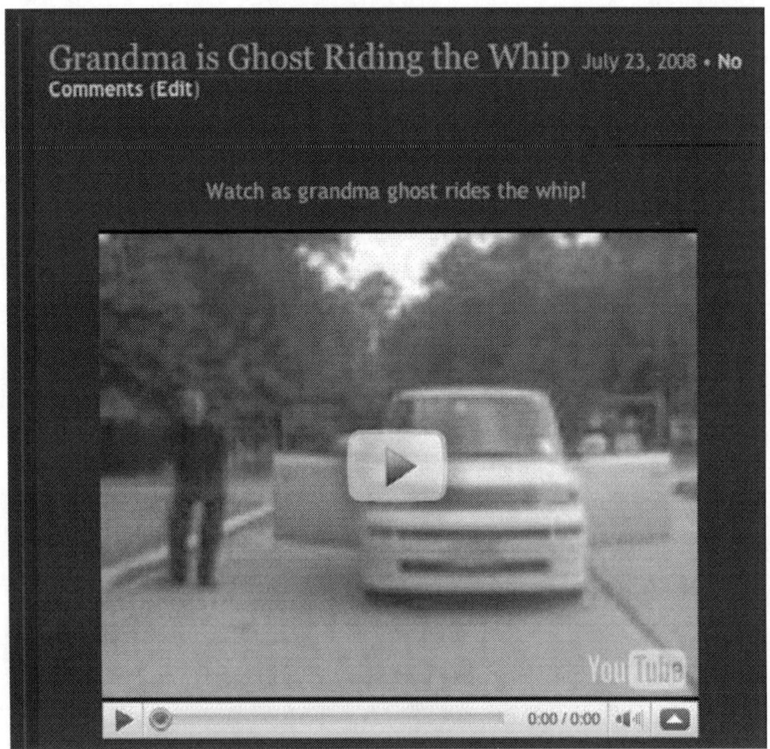

Tip about uploading videos

Whenever you want to share a video, you cannot upload it to your server using wordpress.com, if you have your own server you can, but you need to compress it very highly so it does not take long to download.

A good idea is to go sign up at youtube.com and upload your video there, and then you can link to it here on your blog.

The benefit to this is it eats up YouTube's bandwidth, opposed to your own. They also backup all the videos (and store them in multiple locations on multiple servers) so you don't have to worry about loosing it.

How to add audio to your blog

You have two different ways to add audio to your blog. The first way fixes it so the user clicks a link, and can download the audio, or is launched automatically into the users default Internet audio player. The second way is to "embed" the audio onto your site, and allow users to play your audio via a flash player, while staying on your site.

I prefer both methods, create an audio stream for users to listen to as well as a "download" link.

This is amazing if your creating a blog for your local church or college, as you can have classes posted up and the students can check out the audio from the webpage, without having to download anything, or download it for later study.

To add audio to your site and have a player for them to listen too, type in [audio http://www.domain.com/song.mp3].

While you are writing your post, click insert audio, and type in the following (replace spooky with what matters, I changed it to download).

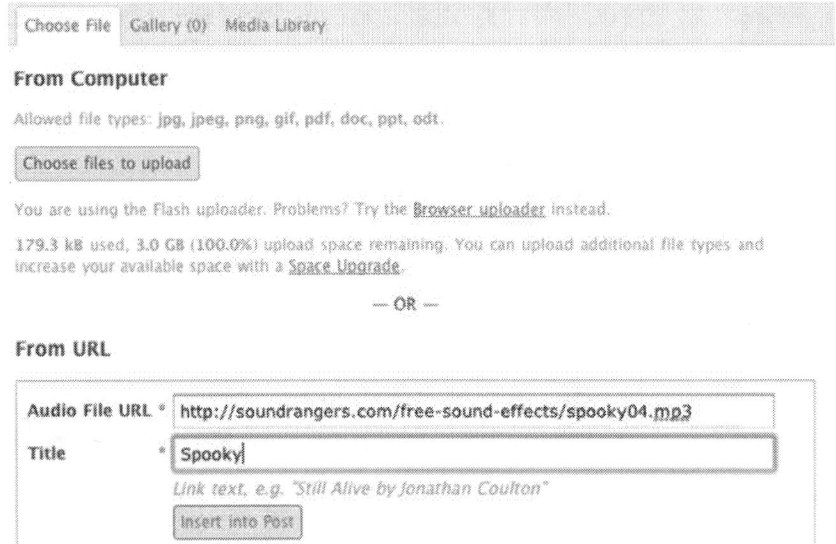

Type this into your blog.

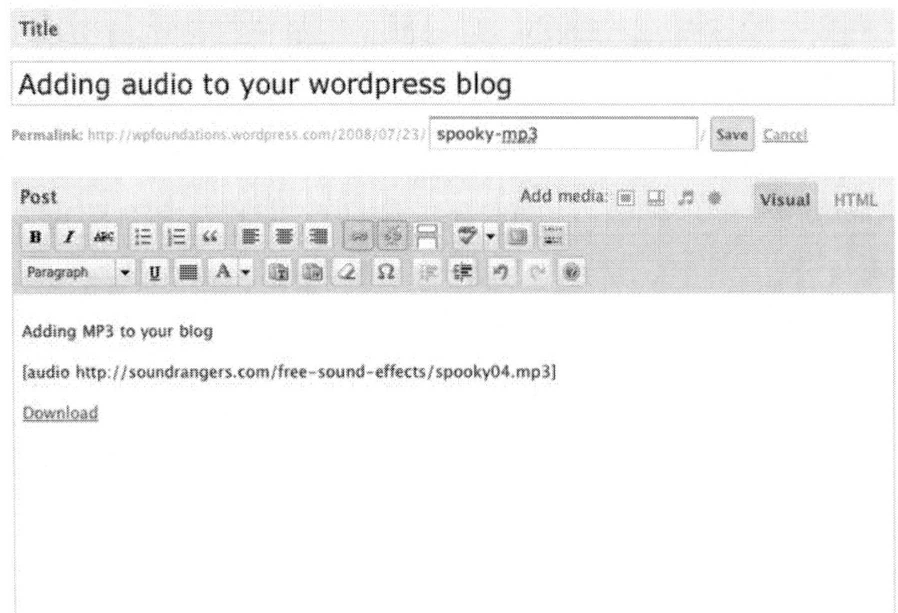

When you are finished, it will look like this when published.

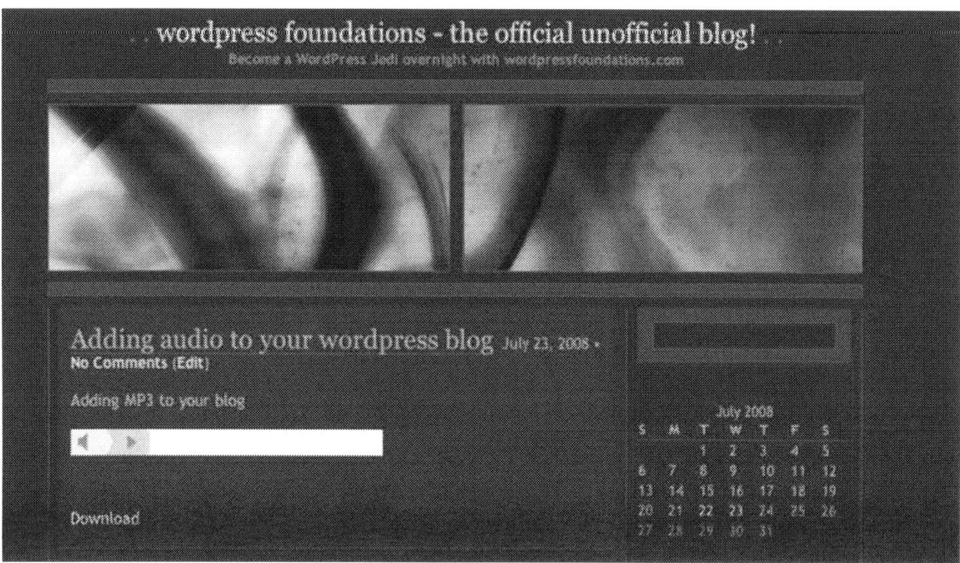

Just as with video, you cannot upload audio to your wordpress.com account. As such you will need to host it on an external server (Amazon s3 is a great place to do this or you can use free webhosting, and link to that file).

Managing your Media Library

When you add images, or other files, WordPress will automatically keep track of them, and organize them. It does not list what you've linked to (images, YouTube videos, mp3's, etc), only that which you personally uploaded, it will show up here.

You can filter, and search by type or name, or delete if you need to free up some space or get rid of duplicate material.

If you click the item, you will see more information about it, and it will show you all the posts the media appears on, and any comments on the item.

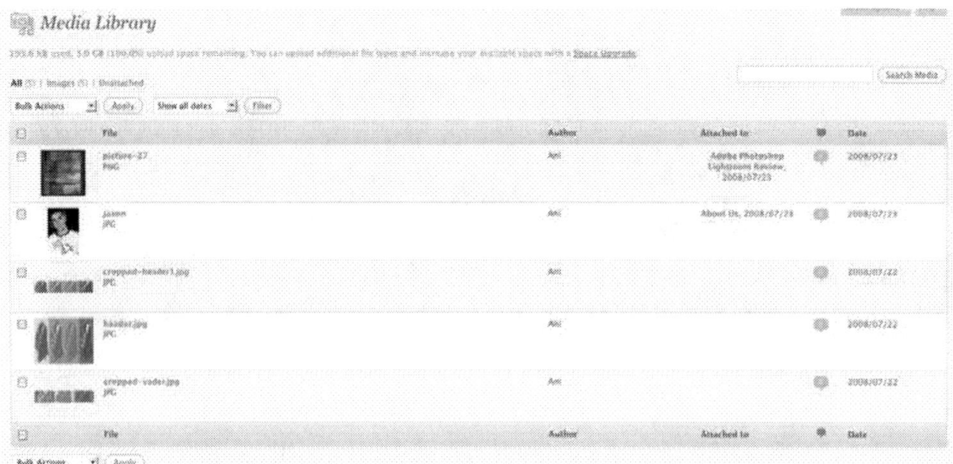

You can add other files on your blog, such as PDF files, or PowerPoint presentations. You add this material the same way you added the other media, the only difference is the file is presented as a download link (like with the audio).

You can access your media library by clicking the Media button on the left hand side menu on your dashboard, and choose Library.

Chapter 15 Summary

In this chapter, we went over how to add multimedia to your blog.

You learned how to add photos (both by linking to an image on another website, such as flickr or Amazon, and by uploading a file from your computer). You learned that you can take advantage of the image hosting services (which were listed in chapter 2) to save on bandwidth and store your multimedia off site.

You learned how to add videos from YouTube to your WordPress.com site. If you're using WordPress.org you need to embed YouTube videos to your site. To do this, you copy the embed code and use HTML mode (when writing text, reference chapter 7 as needed) to paste in the embed code and the video will show up.

I created a comprehensive tutorial on adding videos to your website from YouTube, you can read it here ->

enlightenedwebmastery.com/advanced-youtube-embedding-techniques

Chapter 15 Action Steps

- Add a video from YouTube, add an mp3, as well as some photos.
- Make note of the processes so you can repeat it later on.

Chapter 15 - Adding Multimedia to your blog

Chapter 16

Managing Your Pages and Posts

Introduction to chapter 16

In this chapter you're going to learn about the More Tag as well as the excerpt tag. By using the more tag, when a visitor sees your homepage, they will be presented with a read more option.

By taking advantage of the Excerpt option, you will cut down on duplicate content.

Some themes will display the Excerpt on the home page, others use it in your archives / categories / tag pages.

You will learn how to delete or edit content, as well as some editing strategies.

When you're thinking about deleting a post or page, you need to keep some things in mind.

If other sites are linking to that page, when a visitor finds that link and clicks it, they will see a 404 page, and be unable to view that material.

One way to handle this is to edit the post and include a link to the new material (or code in a redirect), that way they will be able to view the new material.

Another option would be to edit the page, and add an addendum to the bottom of the post telling what's changed.

If the post is something that will be updated frequently, you should be using a Page not a Post, then just edit the Page as needed.

Introduction to the More Tag

In a previous chapter, we posted a long review on our blog. The problem is, when you pull up the website, people have to look at that large body of text, and scroll around. As such they may decide to leave the site than deal with having to view that large body of text. This is where the More Tag comes in.

Have you noticed when you visit a blog, the home page says, to read the rest of the post, click here. This is thanks to using the More Tag.

Applying The More Tag

Go to your dashboard, under Posts, choose Edit, and select a post that has a large body of text.

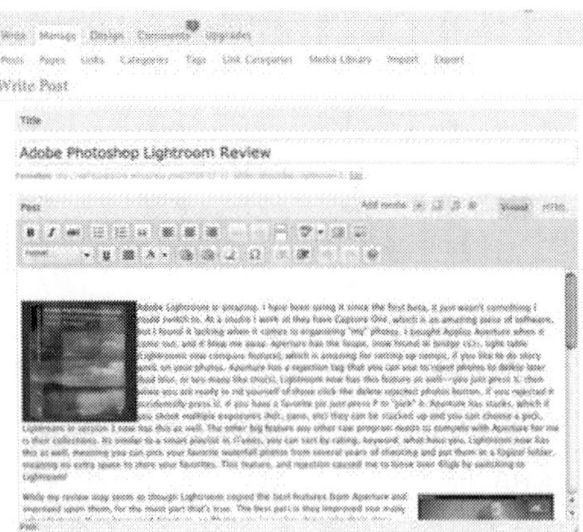

What we need to do now, is write a summary, or a brief introductory paragraph for the article, and follow with the more tag. Think of this as a teaser, it can be as long or short as needed.

The more tag is the first button.

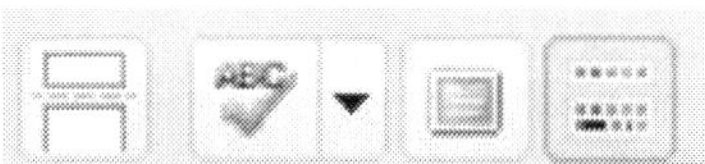

When you're finished click the "more tag" button, you'll see something similar to the graphic below, click save, and visit the site.

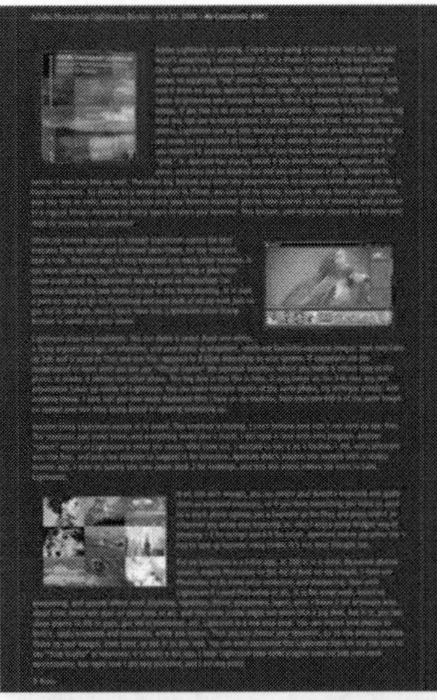

This is what the front page of the blog looked like, prior to implementing the more tag.

I had to make the text extremely small to get it all to fit on my monitor.

Here is what the front-page post now looks like now that we used the more tag:

Adobe Photoshop Lightroom Review July 23, 2008 • **No Comments** (**Edit**)

Hey, I just found this really cool photo editing program. It is made by Adobe (the makers of Photoshop), what it does is organize all of your photos, and lets you work with raw photo files in real time, and allows quick and easy access to manipulate them.

The name of this program is, Adobe Lightroom. I have been using it since beta, and I have to say, it brings serious joy to my life.

The program has a very deep and easy to use "tagging" system, which allows me to sort not only by name, or by a keyword, but I can also search by which lens or camera body, the date, and I can assign a color, and sort by that on an image by image basis. You can sort by ISO, your fstop, or your shutter speed. It is incredible.

Please read on to find out how Lightroom caused me to loose over 40GB of wasted space in under a day!

Continue reading 'Adobe Photoshop Lightroom Review'

Learning how to use the excerpt tag

By using the excerpt tag, (depending on your theme) instead of displaying the beginning of your text, the theme will show your excerpt.

Usually your excerpt will appear under "archives or categories".

Without the excerpt tag when you search by archive, you will still see the introductory post, prior to the more tag, what we need to do now, is write a quick excerpt about the article, so when it's searched for, they see that piece of information opposed to the introduction (especially if it is a long post.)

I like to keep these at around 25 words, very short, and to the point, with keywords so when users are searching, they can easily find the post.

Go back to your dashboard, click manage, then post, and scroll down to bottom of your post. Underneath you'll see excerpt, this is where we'll type in our excerpt.

Here is an example of an appropriate excerpt for this article.

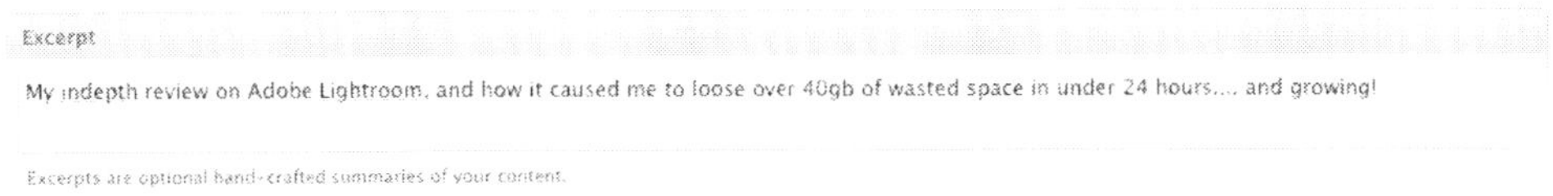

Excerpt

My indepth review on Adobe Lightroom, and how it caused me to loose over 40gb of wasted space in under 24 hours.... and growing!

Excerpts are optional hand-crafted summaries of your content.

How this shows up varies by theme, for example:

Our current theme doesn't display any information when you search, or use the archives, other than the title.

When you switch back to Kubrick, you see what's before the more tag.

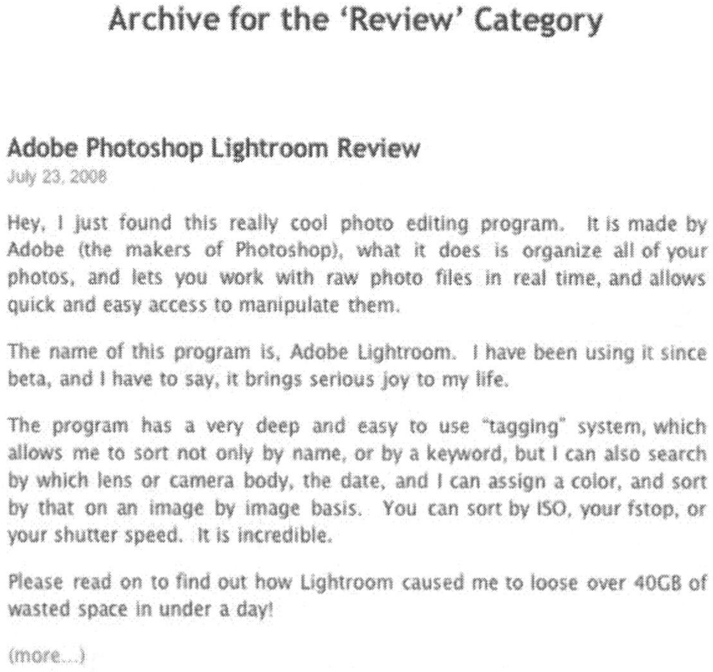

Archive for the 'Review' Category

Adobe Photoshop Lightroom Review

July 23, 2008

Hey, I just found this really cool photo editing program. It is made by Adobe (the makers of Photoshop), what it does is organize all of your photos, and lets you work with raw photo files in real time, and allows quick and easy access to manipulate them.

The name of this program is, Adobe Lightroom. I have been using it since beta, and I have to say, it brings serious joy to my life.

The program has a very deep and easy to use "tagging" system, which allows me to sort not only by name, or by a keyword, but I can also search by which lens or camera body, the date, and I can assign a color, and sort by that on an image by image basis. You can sort by ISO, your fstop, or your shutter speed. It is incredible.

Please read on to find out how Lightroom caused me to loose over 40GB of wasted space in under a day!

(more...)

When you switch to digg 3 columns, you see the excerpt.

Adobe Photoshop Lightroom Review

Posted on **July 23, 2008** by Ani | Edit

My indepth review on Adobe Lightroom, and how it caused me to loose over 40gb of wasted space in under 24 hours.... and growing!

Filed under: Review | Tagged: adobe, lightroom, photoshop, Review | No Comments »

So again, this is based on your theme, but this is such a good habit to get into, that it is worth doing it.

I do not like having duplicate content on my sites, and using the excerpt function, along with the more tag, and having different content on all 3 pages, ensures this is kept to a minimum.

Deleting and Editing Content

In this section we'll cover how to edit our posts.

For example, consider that you run a celebrity gossip site, and some celebrity couple is moments away from having a baby. You can go ahead and write your post, publish it and start getting comments, then later on, when the babies names are announced, you can go back to that post and edit it to include the names.

To do this, you would click edit, select the post, add the new information to the bottom and then click publish and all visitors will now see this new information.

If you wish to delete that post, (maybe it was to crass), visit your dashboard, on the left side menu click edit, then when viewing your posts, check the box and choose delete. You can also hover over the name of the post and click the delete button.

For an example of editing a post, follow along with the following example: Visit Dashboard, click edit, edit a post then follow along.

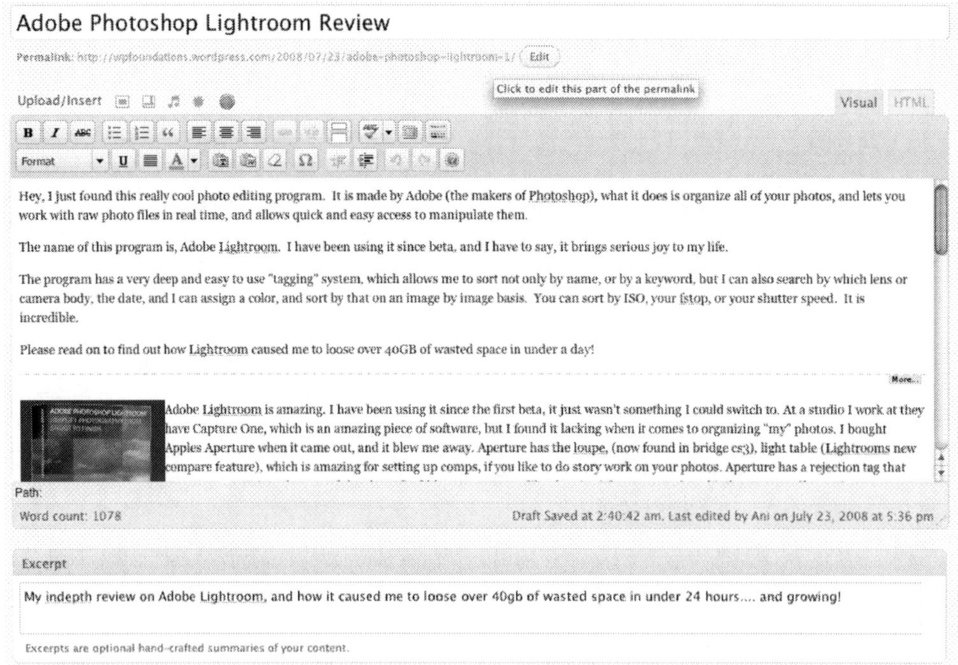

Make your changes to the post (whatever they may be), then read the text and make sure everything is right.

Take the time to read over your entire post, and make sure it covers everything, you see no glaring mistakes, both spelling wise, and grammar wise. Once you're happy, click save. Your post is now edited, and will appear exactly where it was (chronologically).

If you want the edited post to appear as the latest entry on your blog, you need to do the following.

On the right side of your window, where you click save, you will see a dialog box like the one below, all you need to do is adjust the date to the current time, and date, and then click save. The post will magically be brought up to the front of your blog .

When you edit your posts it's a good habit to write on the bottom of the post that you edited it, and why you edited it.

For example you could write:

"UPDATE 9/28/09, Brad Pitt's new kids name is _____.

Be sure to check back on my blog for the latest happenings!

Click this link to read the latest news on this story."

Chapter 16 Summary

In this chapter we covered how to use the more tag and the excerpt tag.

You learned why they are important, and how to start using these tags immediately.

We went over how to delete a post or edit a post (visit dashboard, click edit, then hover over a post and choose edit or delete), and ways to handle editing a post (as well as how to get the edited post to appear at the top of your blog (like if it was new).

Chapter 16 Action Steps

- If you have a lot of content already on your blog, I want you to spend some time editing your posts, go in, add an excerpt to each post.

- If your theme shows the full posts, go ahead and edit each post and write an introduction to the post (think a teaser, this can be anywhere from 20-200 or so words long, make sure it is not the same as your excerpt.

- Whenever you edit a post, give a reason for your edit, and a date so that readers can see that you added new information. You may consider changing the publish date so your readers will know something has been added.

Chapter 17

Categories and Tags

The difference between categories and tags

In this chapter we are going to focus on the differences between categories and tags, and you'll learn how to use and why.

When you're planning out your blog, I want to keep this in mind, [Categories = General, Tags = Specific].

Here is an example for a video gaming blog, please note I'm using game titles as a tag, and a console as a category. If the blog covered PC and Consoles you could create PC as a category, and Console as a parent category with Xbox 360, Playstation 3 or Nintendo Wii as children.

Halo = Tag, Half Life = Tag, Playstation 3 = Category, Webcam = Category.

By following this example, if you visit my blog and see a post about Halo, you can click that tag, and then see more posts on my blog about Halo. If you clicked the category, Xbox, you would see posts that relate to Xbox (including many games opposed to one). This is how you should organize the structure of your blog

Creating Your Categories

Now that you know the difference between the two, it's time to show how to create them in bulk through the dashboard.

Open up your dashboard, click on Posts, then choose categories.

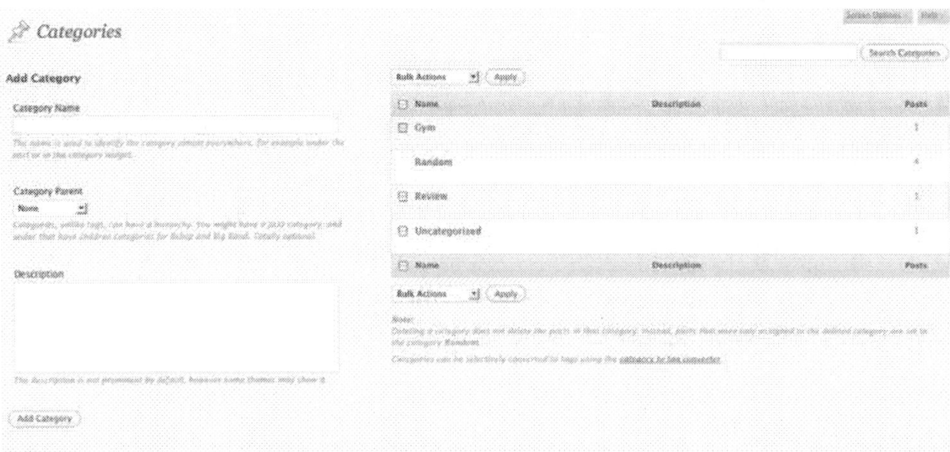

You can see the categories you have on your current blog.

Here's a snapshot of a blog I setup that has descriptive categories, this particular example is for a photography blog. The interface is different because it's using an older version of WordPress, and is self-hosted opposed to ran on wordpress.com.

Take note of the detailed descriptions, and how they relate to the category name. This blog was created before we had tags.

7	Canon	Articles written for or about Canon DSLR's. This will cover guides, faqs, how to's and help.	0	0	Edit	Delete
4	Lightroom	Articles written about Adobe Photoshop Lightroom. These can consist of workflows, tips, guides, as well as FAQS.	0	0	Edit	Delete
8	Photo	This is where I post Photo's. You can view any of my photos that I have posted to the blog. Most will be posted on Flickr, and shown here.	30	0	Edit	Delete
6	Photography	This will cover photographic tips, such as compositing, and helpful ideas.	0	0	Edit	Delete
5	Photoshop	Articles written for Adobe Photoshop. Mainly the current version CS3.	0	0	Edit	Delete
3	Reviews	Reviews of software, hardware, games, books and videos.	0	0	Edit	Delete
1	Uncategorized		0	0	Edit	Default

To add a category, just type in the name, and insert the information presented.

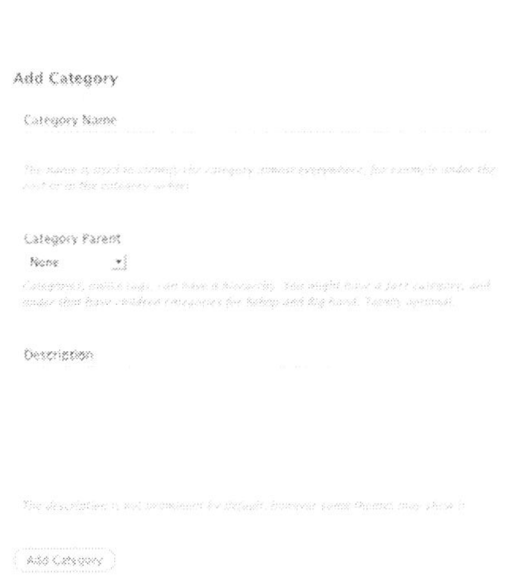

Give your category a name.

Earlier we talked about the differences between tags and categories, and how you should be general in your category name, and much more specific when it comes to tags.

Unlike tags, you will always be able to see the categories you have, as such, try and keep them to a minimum.

The Category Parent is what you would select if you wanted to subdivide your categories.

Earlier in this book I mentioned an example using video games, to continue on in that theme, you could create a "parent category" of "Consoles", and then make children of, Xbox 360, Playstation 3, and Nintendo Wii.

This way, if a user had all three systems, he could select Consoles, and see all your console related news, but if he only had a Wii, he could select that category, and see only Nintendo Wii posts.

Next we need to give a description. Look at the previous picture, and see how the descriptions were made, make it simple, you're not writing an article, try and keep it between one and two sentences.

You can go ahead and create as many categories right now as you want, when you are finished, we will go over tags some more, and show exactly how to manage them, and a cool little tool that can make tags even more fun!

Adding Tags

Adding tags is a very simple process.

From your dashboard, click on Posts, and then select Tags.

Under Publish you'll see the "tags" menu box. Here is where you select your tags.

You really need to try and be consistent; WordPress does not let you visually see all the tags you have on your site while your writing a post.

In keeping with the video game theme, try not to use GTA 4, GTA IV, GTA IV 4, choose one, and stick with it, or use all three if you want, the point is to be consistent, and develop a guideline.

Once you have a guideline for how to create a tag whenever you write a new post, add your tags and follow your guidelines.

Deleting Tags

If your looking over a post, and do not like a certain tag, you can delete it by clicking the x button next to the name.

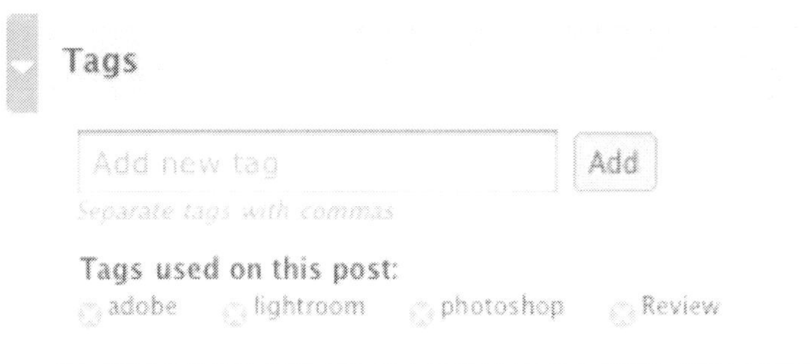

Managing your tags

Consider that you had a blog for a while now, and you're trying to organize your tags. This little sample site we have been creating here, has no purpose, and only a few posts, yet the amount of tags are already becoming unruly. We currently have 15 tags, in as few as three or four posts.

Inside of your dashboard, click on Posts, then choose Tags, and you will see the following screen.

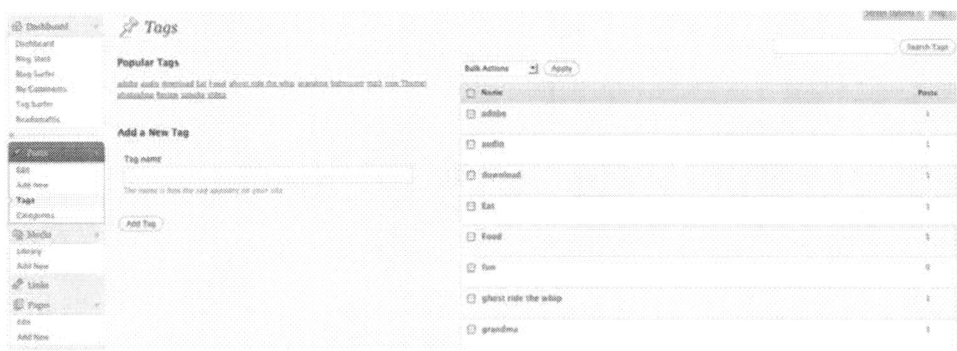

Whenever you click on "quick edit" you can choose to rename your tag, doing so makes changes site wide, so if you accidently misspelled a tag, and have been doing so for quite some time, you can easily change it, and it will be as though it never happened.

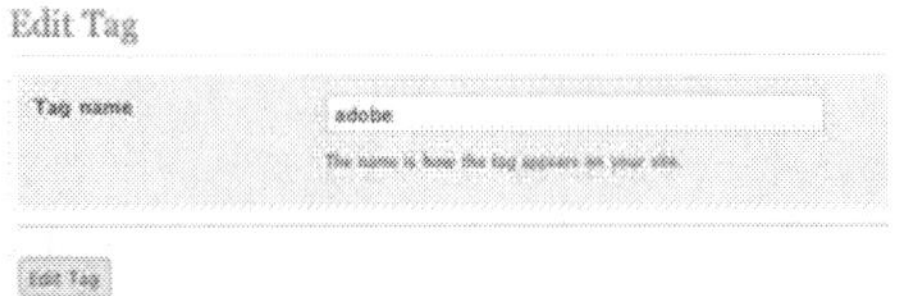

If you decide you no longer want the tag, just delete it, and it's gone. Click the little checkbox, and choose delete (its near the top).

If you want to see all the posts you created that are using that tag, click the number on the right that shows how many posts you have with it, and you'll be presented with a dialog box similar to below.

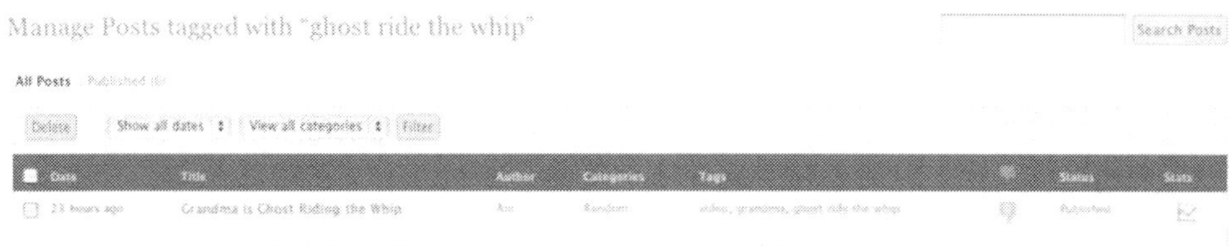

From here you can check your stats, the other tags on that post, and if you have any comments.

Converting your categories to tags

If you have had your WordPress blog for sometime, you may have quite the collection of categories. Thanks to the recent update, you now have tags built in, and after seeing how useful they are, you might want to change your categories to tags.

Doing this is very easy. Load up your dashboard, click on Tools, and choose Import. Then click **Categories to Tags Converter**.

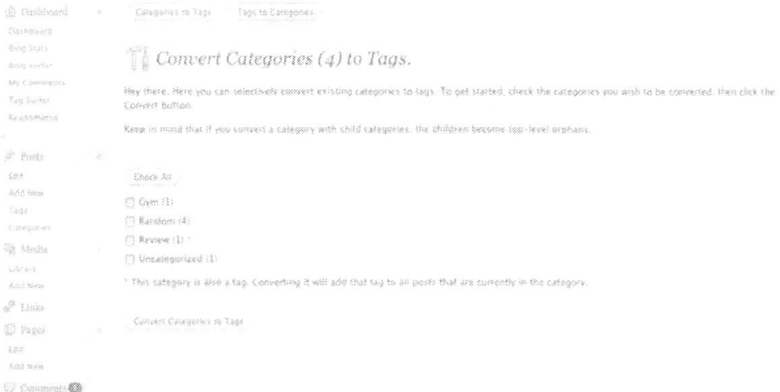

All you need to do is click a category, and select convert selection to tags.

Convert your Tags to Categories

From the same screen as above, select "Tags to Categories".

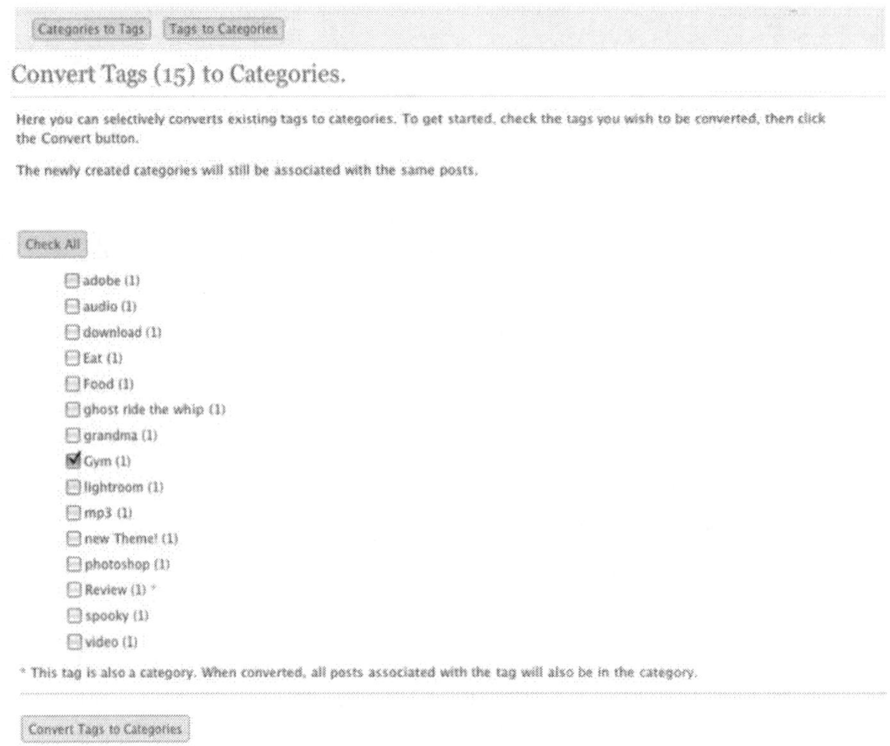

Select the "Tags" you wish to convert into a Category (you can select more than one), and press "Convert Tags to Categories".

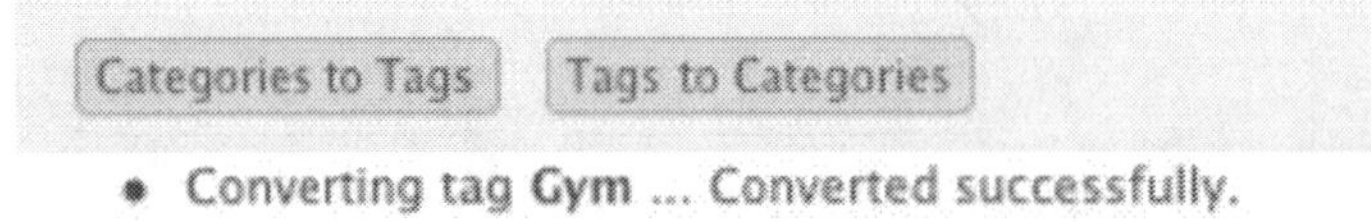

If you find you're constantly using a tag, and you think you should convert it to a category, you now know how.

If you find out your not using as a category as much as you thought you would, you can convert it to a tag or delete it.

Chapter 17 Summary

This chapter taught you the differences between Categories and Tags (Categories = General, Tags = Specific), as well as some workflow tips and techniques (Create a guideline, for example, GTA 4, or GTA-4, or GTA_4, and use it for all your tags.

When you implement this, your site will remain consistent, and you need not reference your tags before you create one (thinking "What did I put the last time I used this tag?").

You also learned how to convert tags to categories and vice versa.

You learned how to create descriptions for your categories as well as how many posts are using to that category.

One last thing to keep in mind is, it's considered a best practice to use only one category when possible. By having one post belong to multiple categories, you're creating duplicate content, and possibly making it confusing to your readers.

By taking full advantage of tags and categories, you can create a better and more cohesive experience for your readers.

Chapter 17 Action Steps

- Take the category list you created in chapter 7, and input those categories using the techniques taught in this chapter (adding a description, and making sure it's appropriate).
- If you have extraneous tags consider deleting them.
- If you think a tag would be a better category, (or vice versa) convert them.
- Devise a guideline for how you'll create tags. By doing this, you will be able to gauge if you have used the tag before, and if you did the post will already be tagged correctly.
- Examples of guidelines: tag, Tag, tag-tag, tag_tag
- After you write a post, and you're not sure if you used the tag prior, check your tags and edit as necessary.

Chapter 18

Adding Users

Introduction to adding users

In this chapter you'll learn how to add users for your blog.

If your blog is only going to be updated by you, you can feel free to skip this chapter.

The benefit of having more than one user on your site is, you don't have to do all the work.

Some example cases where you might want to add users are:

A church blog. You need someone to upload podcasts, someone to update the schedule for the week, a bible quote of the day, activities, and more. You can have one person in charge of each aspect, give them a login, and they can work on it piece by piece.

Another example would be, you have a news blog and you have 3 different people coming in and editing posts. Maybe you hired someone to write for you, and they can login and input their post. By taking advantage of user classes (which we'll talk about next) you can set it up where that user can post, but they post cannot be published.

The Different user classes

I am listing these in order of privileges allowed. From most restricted to least.

Contributor - This guy can login to your blog, write some posts, as well as edit (their own posts), and can upload files to the blog.

They cannot publish their posts; those have to be published by a user of a higher class.

Author - This guy can do everything the contributor can, plus he can publish as well as delete his own posts.

Editor - This guy can do everything the author can, and he can edit other people's posts, publish unpublished posts, edit comments, pretty much everything you would want in regards to managing content. This person needs to be someone you can trust, as he can pretty much control all the content on the blog.

Administrator - He can do any and everything, including deleting the blog. (So be very careful who you add as an Administrator.)

Inviting a user

To invite a user, go to your WordPress dashboard, click the Users option, and choose **invites**. You can choose the class, and decide if you want to add them to your blog roll (list of links you can post on your site), or to add them as a contributor.

Once they get your email, they need to join WordPress, using the same steps we did earlier on in this book.

A screenshot of adding a user

Managing Users

To manage your users, just go to your dashboard, click users. When you do this you will see your users, if you have many users, you can sort by class, or type in their name in the search box.

You can see how many posts they have made, as well as remove them from your blog (click the check box).

If you wish to promote the user, just click their name, and then you can promote or demote them based on the list we discussed earlier.

Chapter 18 Summary

In this chapter we covered how to add users to your blog, and the advantages of doing so, as well as some precautions to take when adding a user to your WordPress blog.

You learned about the different user classes, and how to manage your users (as well as delete them).

Chapter 18 Action Steps

- Come up with a list of names that you'll be adding to your blog.
- Read page 176 and apply a class for each user.
- Then add those users to your site with the appropriate class.

Chapter 19

Password Protection

Why do I want to password protect?

Some reasons you may want to password protect a page are as follows:

- Creating an event you only want select people to know and communicate about.
- A special offer for certain people.
- A promotion.
- You want to sell some information, and have that information given only to those with the password.
- To share embarrassing photos with someone.

What can go wrong using password protection?

As with anything, people like to share. You have to realize that people will share their password with friends, family, or the whole Internet! So do not rely on password protection for something really important.

The way this works is, you create a password, and you give that password out to people. Those people visit your post, and type in the password in order to gain access.

How to protect a page or post using a password

Go to your dashboard, click Pages, then Edit, and choose a Page. At the top where it says Publish, under visibility, select "Password Protected".

Whenever someone visits your site, they will see the title, when they click on it, they will have to type in the password, when they do, they will be able to see the content.

You can still see the Page listed below (About Us). When you click on it, you will be asked to input the password.

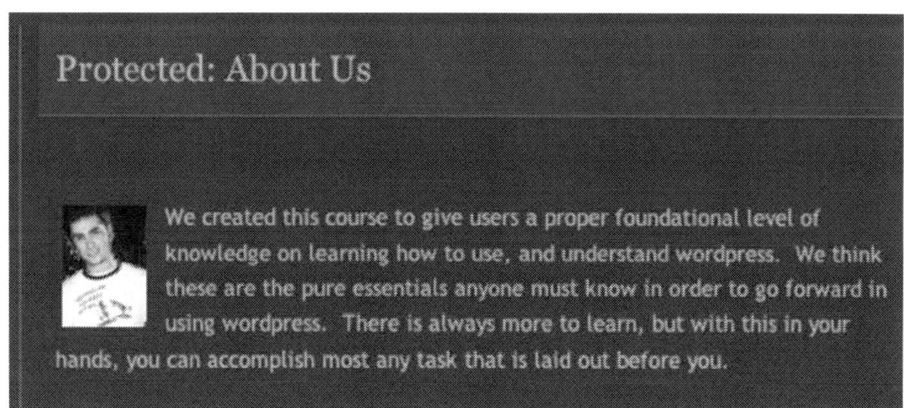
Protected: About Us
We created this course to give users a proper foundational level of knowledge on learning how to use, and understand wordpress. We think these are the pure essentials anyone must know in order to go forward in using wordpress. There is always more to learn, but with this in your hands, you can accomplish most any task that is laid out before you.

When you finish typing in the password, you will be allowed to view the page, as above.

How to get rid of Password Protection

Go back to your dashboard, click manage, and select either page or post depending on what you chose prior, and delete the password from the page.

Now when you view the site, the password is no longer required.

Chapter 19 Summary

In this chapter we talked about Password Protection.

You learned how to enable it for each post, as well as the potential pitfalls of using Password Protection.

If you're wanting to run a membership site then you really want to think about using a third party resource like aMember Pro.

http://www.amember.com/

The product costs (at this time) around 200 dollars, and it is the best, most secure option.

Chapter 19 Action Steps

- Decide if Password Protection is for you
- If it is, when you write a post, keep that password handy so you can send it out to the people who need to access that content.
- If you want to run a membership site, you should consider using aMember.

Chapter 20

Your Blog roll

Introduction to Blog Rolls

So, you may have wondered what a "blog roll" is, and why you have one or need one.

When you find a website you enjoy, and you want to share it with the world, you can add it to your blog roll. Then readers of your blog will see the link, and can decide to check it out. That site may add you to their blog roll as well. It's a great way to communicate with your audience, and helps to grow your community.

You are not stuck to having just one "blog roll", you can create multiple lists that are separate. For example, you can have a list of friends, stores, sites, services, family, etc.

Adding Links

In your dashboard, click on Links (left side menu), then "Add New".

You're given three options. *The Name* (this will show up on your blog roll), *the address* (this needs to be the complete URL including http://), and a *description* (what users will see when they are hovering over your link, provided snapshotz is not enabled).

You can flesh this out, by assigning categories to your links. Make sure you hit save after you add the link.

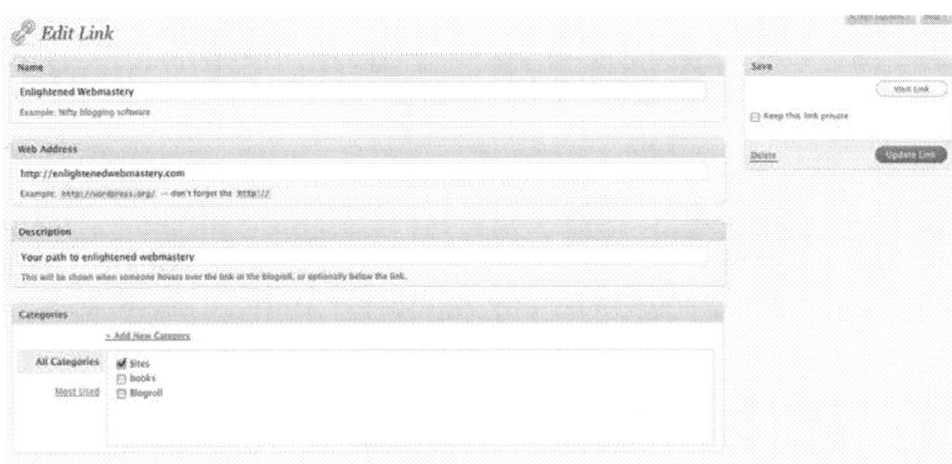

After adding these in, you can see how it looks on your site by clicking visit site (after hitting save).

If you decide you want to delete some links, just go to Links -> Edit, from your dashboard.

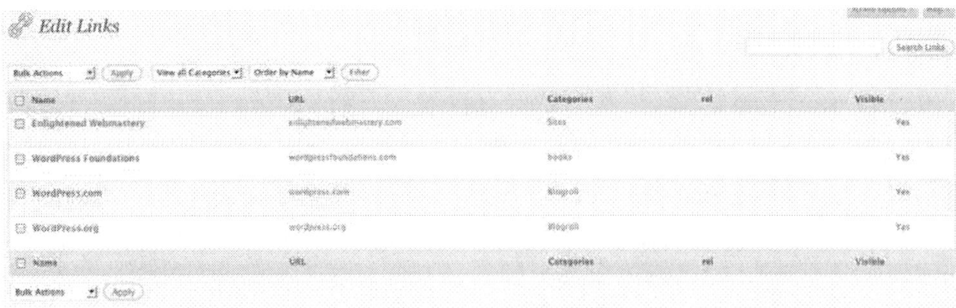

Chapter 21

Maintenance

Introduction To Maintenance

If you are running a business website, where your information is more static than dynamic, you may not need to create much content, as most of your material will be static. For others who are interested in keeping a content filled blog, you need to create some content regularly, as well as do some basic "house keeping".

Posting Content

Google loves sites that have new content. Google actually ranks higher based on the "freshness" of your content. Meaning the more often you update your blog, with valuable content, the more often it will get indexed, and the higher you will rank. This is important, because the higher you are ranked, the more people will be able to view your website and buy whatever your selling, or respond to your latest news articles.

A good rule is to make an update at least once a week if you can, more if possible, but try and be consistent.

When you are first starting out your blog, it's a good habit to post every day for some time (at least a month or so) then you can drop down to 2-3 times a week, you can go lower as needed (but try to at least update once a week), this way your site becomes more valuable, and your readers will thank you.

How can I keep creating fresh content?

People enjoy hearing about the latest news on whatever it is your covering. A good idea would be to keep apprised on the information in your particular community (niche), and providing relevant content as necessary. You can link to other articles on the internet with your thoughts on the article as the post.

Check your comments and trackbacks

Everyday I check my comments and trackbacks (or try to) and I suggest you do the same. This doesn't take as long as you think it may (5-10 minutes, even on a popular blog).

Checking and deleting your spam.

Try and manually delete your spam, check it daily to see what's going on, and be on top of things.

Checking your incoming links.

See who is linking to you, check out their blog, and maybe leave a comment for them to read, or email them to show your appreciation.

Look for news and updates in the WordPress community.

At least once a week, pay attention to the news updates on your dashboard, and see what's going on in the community.

Check your stats.

See how many visitors you're getting, the keywords they searched to come to your site, and the articles they enjoy the most, this way you can adapt to provide better content for your users.

Chapter 22

Self-Hosted Bloggers

Where Do I Get WordPress.org

Visit *wordpress.org*, on the home page you will see a button telling you to download.

What do I need to install it?

You need a web server (hosting account), and you need FTP access to that server.

You need a text editor (to open a php file).

A FTP client to connect to your server (windows users download filezilla, os x users use Cyberduck).

A web browser so you can set up and configure the installation.

How to install wordpress.org in under 5 minutes

If 5 minutes is just too long, skip to page 190 to learn about the 1 click install that takes seconds to do. You just need to be sure your hosting provider offers the 1 click install service.

After you download WordPress, decompress it, and rename the file wp-config-sample.php to wp-config.php, then open it up in your text editor.

Put in your information for your database, ex:

define('DB_NAME', 'WordPress'); // The name of the database define('DB_USER', 'username'); // Your MySQL username define('DB_PASSWORD', 'password'); // ...and password define('DB_HOST', 'localhost'); // 99% chance you won't need to change this value

Proceed with uploading the files to your server.

I.e. If you want it to be yourdomain.com you would upload all the files inside the WordPress directory to your root directory on your server (not the WordPress folder itself), if you wanted it to be in another folder, like yourname.com/blog/ then rename the WordPress folder to blog, and upload the folder to your server.

How to create a MySQL database and user

I'm going to cover how to do this using phpmyadmin.

Login to your phpmyadmin dashboard.

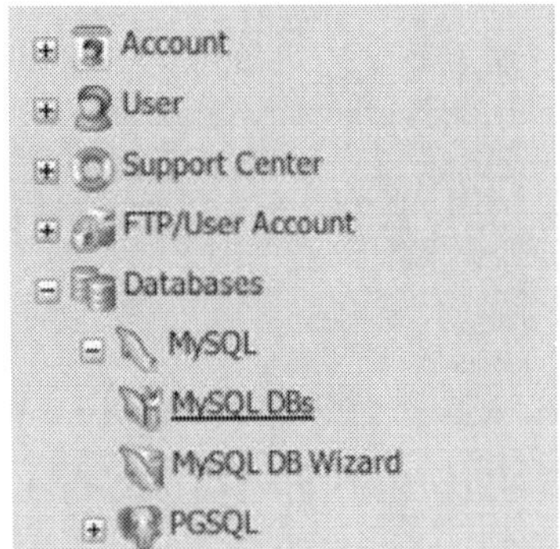

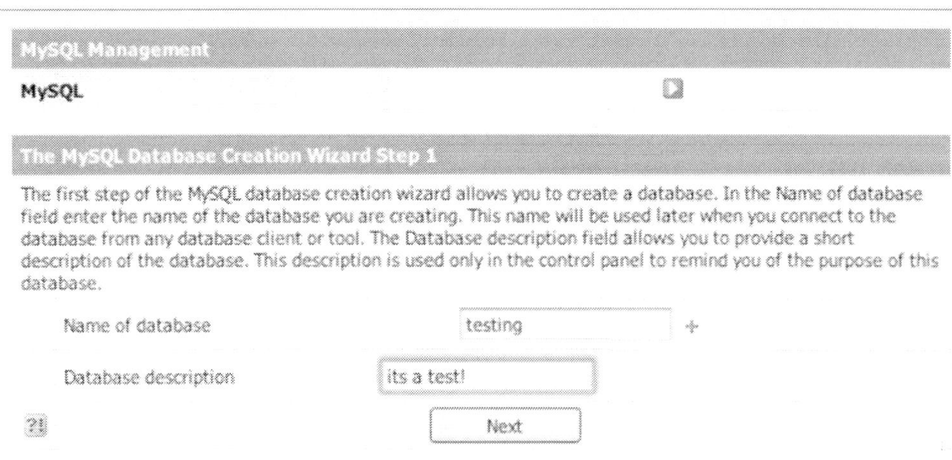
MySQL DB Wizard
MySQL Management
MySQL
The MySQL Database Creation Wizard Step 1
The first step of the MySQL database creation wizard allows you to create a database. In the Name of database field enter the name of the database you are creating. This name will be used later when you connect to the database from any database client or tool. The Database description field allows you to provide a short description of the database. This description is used only in the control panel to remind you of the purpose of this database.
Name of database
testing
Database description
its a test!
Next

Give your database a name (write this down) and give it a description, then click Next.

MySQL DB Wizard

Information: Database _testing has been created successfully

The MySQL Database Creation Wizard Step 2. Adding Users to mistafr_testing

In this step you will add users and set their privileges on the newly created database. In the left part of the form you can add new users. In the right part you can set privileges for already existing users on the newly created database. To add a new user, enter the user login and password, then select a typical role for this user. If you need to set more specific privileges, you can do this from the "MySQL privileges" form later (after the user has been created). To set privileges on the newly created database for an existing user, select this user from the list, then select a typical role of this user and then press the "Add existing user" button. If you need to set more specific privileges on the database, you can do this from the "MySQL privileges" form later.

Add MySQL user to the database mistafr_testing

User name: itsauser

Password: ******

Confirm password: ******

User role: read/write

Add user

Finish

Give yourself a username and password, write these down, as you need to add these to your wp-config.php file.

Now you can upload your file via FTP.

If you get a database error problem, you need to edit your profile, your hostname might need to be changed, or you could have mistyped something. You might need to change the permissions on your server.

1 Click Install

Some hosting providers (such as HostGator or GoDaddy) offer 1 click installs of WordPress. If your hosting provider offers this, follow their directions (and click a button), then your site will be up and running in minutes. Fantastico is the name of the package most sites use to automate WordPress installations. If the previous section seemed confusing, consider looking for a host that offers 1 click installs.

Where to get free themes for your blog

As of July 18th, WordPress is bringing back the theme database, and is now open for new submissions; expect to see it grow astronomically.

Check it out here - *http://wordpress.org/extend/themes/*

When you search for a theme, you will see something similar to the following:

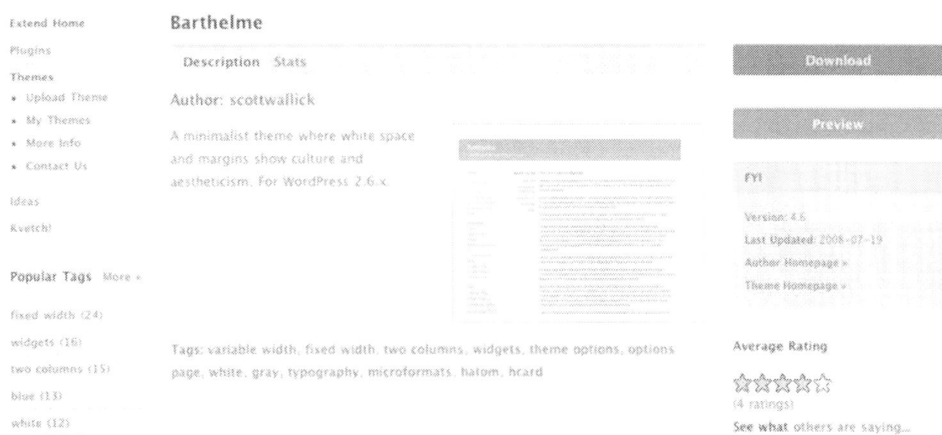

If the screenshot interests you, click on "Preview" and you get to see it live. If you like it, click "download".

How do I install themes?

Once you have the file downloaded, you can decompress it, and get in your ftp program, login, go to your wp-content folder, and you put your theme folder under themes, if it requires plugins you put those plugins in the plugins folder.

Make sure you upload the folder, not the root directory (files).

Once the theme has been uploaded to your site, visit your dashboard, and under appearance you have an option called "Themes". Click that button and you will be presented with a list of all your uploaded themes. To activate the theme, just click on the name, and choose activate. The theme is applied instantly.

Chapter 22 Summary

In this chapter you learned how to install WordPress.org using phpmyadmin. You also learned that you can take advantage of services like Fantastico to do 1 click installations of WordPress (make sure your hosting provider offers this service).

You learned how to install themes (by uploading them to the wp-content folder under themes, then visiting dashboard and clicking themes, then activating the theme.)

Chapter 22 Action Steps

- Choose a hosting provider and install WordPress
- If the process seems complicated, consider using a hosting provider that offers 1 click installs. (Hostgator, GoDaddy).
- Download some themes that look pleasing to you. (check out chapter 9 for more information on themes.)
- Continue on with the book (Chapter 23 or Chapter 5)

Chapter 23

Where To Go From Here

Continuing Your Journey

By now you know how to get your blog up and running. You know how to make posts, you have a schedule for when to do what to keep your blog healthy. You know how to change themes. Basically, you know all you really need to know to use WordPress.

You may be wondering what's next, how can I take my newfound skills, enhance them, and start making a profit, or getting more and more traffic to my website.

The only thing you really need to concern yourself with now is Blogging Strategies, and some more advanced techniques for "Mastering The Web", such as SEO, PPC, content creation, lead generation, Analytics, optimization, and more.

Introducing Enlightened WebMastery

The point behind Enlightened WebMastery, is for me to take what I have spent "YEARS!" of my life learning, and thousands of dollars on learning, narrowing it down into something you can apply right away, and get results. Without requiring you to go through the same pain, getting ripped off, or having to be afraid of not knowing which way to go next (and usually end up going nowhere).

WordPress Foundations is our first publication. The purpose behind it was to provide a solid, up to date, foundational level knowledge of the WordPress platform, as well as giving you some tips and ideas on blogging as a medium.

With this book out of the way, more content will be coming out soon to help you in your newfound business.

We will be covering the various ways to get massive amounts of traffic to your website, leveraging the hottest technologies on the web.

We will be covering tools you can use to make small changes that make big impacts on your website.

WordPress Foundations The Course

WordPress Foundations the course takes what is taught here, and goes a lot more in depth. I wanted to keep this book focused on getting your site up and running, as quickly, and easily as possible.

If you buy this book from Amazon, I will offer you a **special discount** to upgrade to the course. WordPressFoundations.com is the site, after you checkout the site, and see if it is for you, type in:

www.wordpressfoundations.com/amazon

When you do this, you will get the course for a cheaper price. The difference between the two is the Amazon link will not include the book, so you still need this printed book. (The course **assumes** you have the book, and you do need it to complete the course, as I do not repeat most of the stuff covered in the book).

The course has several components.

You get a **quick start study guide**. This is based on the structure of how I would go about talking with you in real life. I would ask you questions, and have you make decisions based on the answer.

Each chapter has its own set of "**Action Steps**" that you can take that will REALLY get you ahead of the game. If you have no clue what your blog is about, you really should be checking out the videos.

You also get the **Videos**, of me going through a lot of this information, telling you what each chapter is about prior to reading it, things to look out for, and what you should do to get the MOST out of each chapter. You also get this in **AudioBook** format.

You will get to see videos of me going over different sections of WordPress, covering many of the topics covered here, but in **video format with me teaching you** while I got over the different interface options in real time. This should increase your ability to move around 10x.

My favorite part about the course is, I go over some more **advanced techniques**, and things that you REALLY need to know and get handled. (In both **video, and written worksheets**)

I cover **advanced content creation strategies**, showing you how to come up with ideas for your blog, how to structure them, and exploit them to your advantage so you will never be stuck trying to "think up something to say" again.

One of my favorite parts of the course is SEO (**Search Engine Optimization**). I teach you how to install a SEO plug-in, and take full advantage of it. SEO is a very advanced concept. If you hired a "real" SEO off elance.com or a firm, meaning someone who does it professionally (not some guy who read a book), it will typically run you about $1,500 for that person to look at your site, write down some suggestions, and send you the bill. I will be covering what that would typically cover in this course. I will also show you HOW to change these things. (Which could cost you so much more)

This is not going to be super in-depth, you do not NEED to know everything, but what I do cover, you REALLY need to know. It will be similar to this course. I will teach you what you need to know, without boring you to tears with technical mumbo jumbo (and trust me, SEO is FILLED with technical mumbo jumbo).

Your Free Bonuses

Do not forget to visit *EnlightenedWebmastery.com* and sign up for our newsletter, so you can get a free 15-20-page report on manipulating graphics online, as well as updates to this book.

If you would like to see something covered in more detail, do not be afraid to ask, I am very interested in your feedback. Contact me.

NOTES

Write down your account information, usernames, passwords, emails, URLs, for your hosting providers, blog, databases, etc. As well as the name of your site for reference.

If you do not wish to write it here, please write it on a 3.5-inch card and keep it with you, so you can keep track later on should you need to change something.

Made in the USA